trotman

GETTING INTO

Psychology

5th Edition

James Burnett & Maya Waterstone

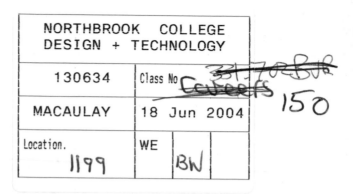
Getting into Psychology
Fifth edition

First published in 1994; second edition 1996; third edition 1999; fourth edition 2002; this fifth edition published in 2004 by Trotman and Company Ltd
2 The Green, Richmond, Surrey TW9 1PL

© Trotman and Company Limited 2004

Editorial and Publishing Team
Authors James Burnett and Maya Waterstone
Editorial Mina Patria, Editorial Director; Rachel Lockhart, Commissioning Editor; Anya Wilson, Editor; Erin Milliken, Editorial Assistant.
Production Ken Ruskin, Head of Pre-press and Production
Sales and Marketing Deborah Jones, Head of Sales and Marketing
Managing Director Toby Trotman

British Library Cataloguing in Publication Data
A catalogue record for this book is available from the British Library

ISBN 0 85660 950 1

Typeset by MacStyle Ltd, Scarborough, N. Yorkshire

Printed and bound in Great Britain by Creative Print & Design (Wales) Ltd

CONTENTS

For up-to-date information on psychology courses
go to www.mpw.co.uk/getintopsych

PREFACE

For 2002 entry, there were about 13,500 applications for psychology courses, of which about 85 per cent were successful. The number of applications has increased enormously over the last fifteen years, and applicants need to think carefully about what strategies they are going to adopt in order to maximise their chances of getting a place to study psychology, and to also ensure that it is at one of their chosen universities. The most popular universities, in particular, are heavily oversubscribed and it is increasingly becoming apparent that the choice of university plays an important part in graduates' job opportunities. The purpose of this book is to give you an overview of the admissions process, from choosing the right course and universities, through to making a convincing and successful application.

We are grateful for the help provided by Trotman & Company who allowed us to bring the information that we had prepared over a number of years for MPW students to a wider readership, and to those who worked on the earlier editions. Thank you also to the British Psychological Society whose excellent website and range of publications made the job of writing this guide much easier, and to UCAS.

James Burnett & Maya Waterstone
November 2003

ABOUT THIS BOOK

Deciding what to study after A-levels is a daunting task. There are already numerous books, guides and leaflets available to help you make your choice. So, why bother to write yet another? *Getting into Psychology* is, as the title suggests, specifically for people wanting to do psychology at degree level. We hope it provides a clear and concise introduction to a subject which relatively few students do at school. It contains information on entry requirements, the length and content of the various courses on offer, and a little about the actual university psychology departments. It also provides some guidelines on filling in section 10 of your UCAS form and preparing for an interview. If, after reading the following chapters, your decisions have been eased in any way, we will have achieved our goal.

It is intended to complement, not replace, existing publications, many of which are included in the reading list at the end of the guide.

Details of entry requirements, courses, campus facilities, etc are constantly changing, and, although the details in this guide are correct at the time of going to press, it is essential to check with UCAS and/or particular universities if you have any queries.

**For up-to-date information on psychology courses
go to www.mpw.co.uk/getintopsych**

INTRODUCTION

It is important to distinguish between the role of the psychologist and other professionals carrying out related work.

- **Psychiatrist**
  A medically trained doctor who chooses to specialise in mental health by taking the membership examinations of the Royal College of Psychiatry. As a consequence of their medical training, psychiatrists can prescribe drug treatments. They will often work as part of a team with clinical psychologists.

- **Psychotherapist**
  Works with both individuals and groups to provide long-term therapy. They will often encourage clients to reflect on their past experience and early development. In theory, graduates of any subject can become a psychotherapist by taking a lengthy training programme of supervised clinical practice and seminars and, in addition, undergoing personal therapy themselves.

- **Psychoanalyst**
  Bases his or her work on Freudian theory and tries to unearth the influence of the unconscious on clients' behaviour. Psychoanalysts work with individual clients in private practice rather than in paid employment. As with psychotherapy, the training period of at least four years includes the process of personal analysis.

Psychology, the study of people and how they act and think, is an increasingly popular subject of study with over 100 higher education institutions offering degree-level courses in the subject either as freestanding degree programmes in their own right or as modules in other combined programmes. Despite this growth in student places, there are still, however, some popular misconceptions about the content of degree programmes. They do not offer students the chance to spend three years studying the works of Freud. Nor do they enable you to see into other people's innermost thoughts.

On the contrary, psychology is taught as a scientific subject and students spend most of their time studying the results of research into human behaviour and the theories which are based on experimental findings. The aim of this introductory chapter is to give you an insight into some of the typical psychological research findings you are likely to study in the course of a degree programme. For more information about psychology as a career, you should look at the British Psychological Society's (BPS) website: www.bps.org.uk.

HOW LONG IS A PIECE OF STRING?

In 1955, the psychologist Solomon Asch set up an experiment in which he sat a group of people around a table and asked them, in turn, to state which of three lines (drawn on one card) was the same length as the single line shown on another card. So, A, B or C?

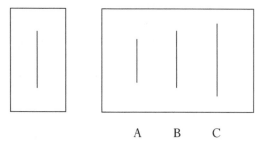

A   B   C

The answer is not as easy as it seems. In fact, the experiment was arranged so that all but one of the group were told beforehand to give the same, but incorrect, answer (ie A). The other person, the 'naive subject' who was not in on the act, was placed to answer last. Surprisingly, despite the simplicity of the task, the naive subject often gave the same wrong answer as his or her companions, preferring to conform than to stand out. It's amazing what peer pressure can do! 'So what?' I hear you cry, 'No one goes round asking complete strangers to judge the lengths of lines.'

In subsequent experiments, Asch found that the naive subject's response often varied with the composition of the group. If one other person deviated from the general consensus (even if he or she gave the other wrong answer), then the subject usually gave the correct response. If the subject was allowed to write his or her judgement on paper, the answer was always right and, if someone left the room before responding, the subject felt able to give the right answer (assuming, no doubt, that the absent person would have given the correct reply).

It seems, therefore, that a person's expressed thoughts and opinions are not necessarily what he or she secretly believes. The study was deliberately designed to be simple and unlike anything the naive subjects had previously experienced so that they could not refer to past events to guide their behaviour. In addition, there was no risk of some members being thought of as more 'expert' than others in the field of judging line length!

Therefore, if peer pressure could have such a profound effect in this simple task, imagine the implications for real life situations. Many other researchers did similar studies, finding that the results varied according to factors such as, how the subject rated his or her companions, whether the subject wanted to be accepted by them and wished to conform, or whether the subject felt superior to them and didn't care that they might be ridiculed for deviating from the general judgement, and so on.

NOW YOU SEE IT...

A good deal of experimental research in psychology has centred on the theme of perception in order to explain how we see and hear. One particular challenge facing psychologists was to account for the way visual illusions, such as the Muller-Lyer illusion below, achieve their effect. Why, for example, does the vertical line in A look longer than that in B?

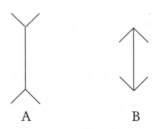

A   B

How can the brain interpret one set of signals in two different ways? One explanation, offered by a researcher called RL Gregory, suggests that the context in which a signal is seen, as well as one's expectations, are both highly influential in the interpretation of sensory signals (visual, audio and tactile). So, if a signal is incomplete, the gaps are filled by what you expect to see, hear or touch, rather with what is really there. Research into this can provide valuable information on how perception normally happens and allows exploration of what can go wrong.

Again, there are far-reaching applications of the findings of such work. For example, if perception is influenced by suggestion and expectation, the gaps filled by the probable rather than the definite, surely the same is true of memory, raising the question: 'How reliable is eye-witness evidence?' Then there is the issue of artificial perception and intelligence – can a computer think or is it only as clever as the person who programmes it?

Coming back to the lines, the way they appear is all to do with perspective. We are fooled into thinking that the 2D image on paper is a 3D phenomenon. Think of it in terms of a room. The vertical line in A is the far corner of a room and the diagonal lines represent the ceiling coming towards us. The diagram in B also shows the corner of a room, but this time it's the corner closest to us and the diagonal lines are the ceiling receding into the distance. Now, because the line in A represents a corner further away from us than the line in B, our brain amplifies the image falling on the retina of the eye to compensate for the extra distance, making it look longer than the line in B which is not amplified. It's a bit like when you see a car on the horizon: you know that it looks tiny because it is a long way away and your brain makes the necessary adjustment to make it look 'car-sized'.

Therefore, perspective is normally useful to us, but the illusion arises if we use it when it is not needed (line A is NOT further away than line B). It's complicated but it is a handy tool to have; artists, architects and designers all make use of it when depicting 3D things on a flat piece of paper. Perspective is, however, a learned process. People who are deprived of seeing things in the distance – like some forest-dwelling tribes and those held in captivity for long periods – do not see things in perspective and, to them, both lines would look the same length.

IT'S NOT WHAT YOU SAY, IT'S THE WAY THAT YOU SAY IT

Verbal communication is interesting for two reasons. Firstly, in association with the theories of speech: how do we learn? Do we plan exactly what to say before we say it or do we put the finishing touches to grammar and word order as we go along? (Think about the errors of speech, how we stumble over words, say them in the wrong order and then go back to make corrections, how we use plural verbs with a singular subject, and so on.) Those 'ums' and 'ahhhs' so common in everyday speech are pauses that allow planning time for the next segment of the sentence.

Secondly, in the way a message is given. How, and by whom, it is delivered can be as influential as its content. For example, is it more effective to speak first or second in a debate? Will the voters remember more of what they heard first or of what they heard most recently? Indeed, do political campaigns really make a difference to voting behaviour? Is an attractive person more likely to be believed than a less attractive one? If not, perhaps spending so much money on media image is a waste of time. Maybe a voter will assure each party that it can rely upon his or her support, reserving his or her choice for the privacy of the polling booth (remember Asch and his lines)? The list is endless!

HOW DO CHILDREN THINK?

Swiss psychologist Jean Piaget earned international renown for his studies of children's intellectual development. As a result of his observations of their behaviour, he suggested that each child goes through a sequence of developmental stages up to the age of 12. One particular experiment characterised the child's thought processes at an early stage of their development and illustrates the process Piaget referred to as 'conservation'.

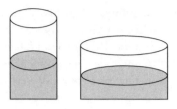

During the experiment he showed a child two identical glasses with equal amounts of liquid and asked the child to agree that they were the same in volume. Piaget then poured the liquid into glasses of different sizes, one tall and thin and the other shorter and wider than the other. Typically the pre-school child no longer agreed that the two glasses contained equal amounts of liquid, arguing that the taller glass had more liquid. At this stage in its cognitive development, the child centres on the appearance of the objects rather than accepting that the volume of the liquid is conserved.

This is simply one example of a lifetime of research into child development undertaken by Piaget. Some of his findings have been challenged by later researchers who have shown that infants in particular are more skilled, cognitively, than Piaget suggested. His ideas, however, have proved highly influential in showing the way that children's thought processes develop over time and have been widely incorporated into the training of teachers and educational psychologists.

If you are keen to find out more, there is a huge array of excellent introductory books on psychology, which will provide an overview of the subject as a whole.

WHY IS PSYCHOLOGY SO POPULAR?

Overall, then, why is psychology such a popular subject for a first degree? There are several reasons.

- Potential students are attracted to a subject that gives them insights into human behaviour and most students of psychology have a basic interest in people.
- It is a particularly attractive subject for mature students who may already have touched on the subject during previous training. Business managers, nurses and social services staff may

well have been introduced to some of the basic concepts in psychology and want to learn more.

■ Psychology is a subject that can be seen to span both arts and science subjects. It attracts students who have broadly based interests and abilities, who do not want to be seen as either an 'arts' or a 'science' person.

■ Finally, although the subject of psychology has been studied at university level for a century – the first professor of psychology was appointed in 1919 – it is still seen as a comparatively 'new' subject and because of the volume of research carried out around the world, students will be studying a subject in which the boundaries of knowledge are constantly changing.

What is more, as a result of the diverse applications of psychology in, for example, healthcare, sports psychology and organisational development, many new and exciting work opportunities are being created.

1

Degree programmes in psychology

When choosing a degree course in psychology there are several points to bear in mind. Firstly, degree programmes will vary in their emphasis. Some will offer a general but comprehensive grounding in the subject. Others will tend to specialise in one branch of psychology. Secondly, admission to courses is usually open to students irrespective of the AS- or A-level subjects or other qualifications they have studied. However, some courses which lead to a Bachelor of Science (BSc) degree in psychology may favour students with science subjects, because of the scientific or experimental nature of the degree course and the ancillary or minor subjects you may be expected to take.

Degree programmes leading to a Bachelor of Arts (BA) degree may look favourably at applicants with arts A-level subjects. The distinction between the two is an important one, because the titles of the awards may not only reflect differences in main course content but also in the choice of subsidiary courses you can take. Those studying for science-based courses may have option choices in neuroscience or physiology whereas those on arts-based programmes may have options in social or developmental psychology.

GENERAL OR SPECIALISED?

Not all first degree programmes in psychology have the same aims. Some are intended to be general in nature, giving a broad and comprehensive overview of all aspects of psychology. Others, by contrast, will attempt to give a special emphasis to one aspect of the subject. You will soon see from the course listings which follow whether a course has a general or specific emphasis. Examples of specialised courses include applied psychology, experimental psychology, occupational psychology and social psychology. There can be some benefits in completing this kind of degree particularly if you already know that this aspect of psychology interests you. On graduation, it may also enable you to gain advanced recognition by the relevant professional group or division of the British Psychological Society.

SINGLE SUBJECT, JOINT OR MODULAR?

Most university departments of psychology will offer a single Honours degree in the subject which means that your principal subject is psychology but that you may have to study other minor subjects in addition, which carry less weight in terms of marks and assessment.

In addition, there are numerous examples of joint Honours degrees in which you study psychology and one other subject to the same level. Examples include Psychology and Management, Psychology and Mathematics, Psychology and Sociology. This kind of programme enables you to study two subjects in depth, but you may need to check whether the overall workload is slightly higher than studying for a single Honours degree.

By contrast, modular degrees offer a range of different subject modules often linked by a unifying theme. Often called 'combined degrees' they are typically provided by institutes and colleges of higher education and enable students to study psychology alongside other subjects in the social sciences or humanities. With joint degrees, and combined degrees in particular, it is important for applicants to check to see if the degree course is recognised by the British Psychological Society (BPS) and gives the Graduate Basis for Registration (GBR). Without this, it will be difficult to qualify professionally. The British Psychological Society's website provides an on-line search for accredited degree courses. The address is given at the back of the book.

FULL TIME OR SANDWICH?

Most degree courses in psychology are full time and last for three years, but some last four years, particularly those in Scotland where it takes four years to gain an Honours degree. A small number of programmes, called sandwich courses, give students the chance to spend their third year on practical placements in companies or with different psychological services or agencies. Students then return to their university for their final year of study.

Although sandwich courses last four years, they can provide students with a valuable opportunity to gain first-hand experience which not only helps them to develop new skills but also to make decisions about which career path to take when they graduate. In one or two instances courses have a 'year abroad' option and arrange for students to spend a year studying at a university outside the UK, in Europe or North America for example.

DEGREE COURSE CONTENT

Most degree courses offer a broad-based introduction to the subject to allow for the fact that many students will not have studied psychology before. This will be followed by increasing specialisation and advanced study as the programme progresses.

FIRST YEAR
In the first year you will be offered introductory courses in different aspects of psychology as well as those in research methods, statistics and the use of information technology. You will hear about some of the key debates in the field of psychological research. For example, how far is human behaviour learned or inherited?

SECOND YEAR
Courses in year 2 will build on and extend subjects studied in the first year. You may also have to complete a series of laboratory or experimental classes to give you a practical insight into psychological research methods. The results of your second year assessment may well count towards your final degree result.

THIRD / FINAL YEAR
In the final year of a degree programme, students usually have the opportunity to choose modules or options that interest them, options which typically reflect the research interests of the staff in the Department of Psychology concerned. At the same time

students will invariably undertake a major dissertation, based on a research project of their own choosing. This is a significant piece of work and the choice of topic may well have some direct relevance to a student's future career choice.

A typical course programme might consist of:

1st year	2nd year	3rd year
Methods and approaches to psychology	Research methods	Research project
Experimental psychology	Further experimental psychology	Option topics
Statistical methods	Behavioural psychology	
Social psychology	Cognitive psychology	
Memory	Developmental psychology	

DEFINITIONS

For potential students who have not studied psychology before, the following definitions may be helpful in knowing what might be covered in different course modules:

Cognitive psychology covers the relationship between the brain and human behaviour. It includes the study of memory, thinking and problem-solving.

Clinical and abnormal psychology concerns the symptoms, classification and theories of different forms of mental illness.

Developmental psychology is the study of the process of human growth and development from birth to adulthood.

Neuropsychology looks at the way the central nervous system operates in relation to the sensory processes – seeing and hearing, in particular.

Psycholinguistics involves the interface between psychology and language, its acquisition and structure.

Psychometrics is the measurement of attributes such as aptitude or personality using psychological tests.

If you want to find out more, you can read one of the introductory textbooks designed for first year undergraduates. As well as the topics listed above you may find that a first degree in psychology will also cover some or all of the following:

- social psychology
- language acquisition
- individual differences and psychological testing
- statistics and experimental methods.

ENTRY GRADES

As with other degree subjects, the grades required for entry to degree courses in psychology vary from one university to another. Typically, the older established universities may ask for 300–340 points, or a grade equivalent (BBB to AAB). By contrast, some of the newer universities may have slightly lower entry requirements. Given the statistical component of most degree courses admissions tutors will also expect applicants to have a reasonable pass grade in GCSE Mathematics.

Further details about the grades required by different universities can be found in some of the university and college listings (page 35).

CHOOSING A UNIVERSITY

With over 100 universities offering psychology and psychology-related courses, how do you narrow down your choice to the maximum of six allowed on the UCAS form?

Things to consider:

- The grades that you are likely to achieve – there is no point in applying to universities whose standard offers are significantly higher than the grades that you are predicted, or get.
- The location of the university.
- The facilities.
- The course.

You might also find it helpful to look at the league tables compiled by the national newspapers. Whilst all league tables should be used as a guide rather than as the definitive ranking of the university, they can be useful as a starting point if you are unsure how to start looking. The *Guardian* newspaper's rankings (http://education.guardian.co.uk/universityguide), in the 2002 table, placed Cambridge first, followed by York, Reading, Loughborough and Oxford. The ranking is based on a number of scores, including a government teaching score, spending, student:staff ratio, job prospects and reputation. The *Guardian* tables can be adapted to suit your own personal weightings: if you wish to produce, for example, a ranking based only on teaching score and reputation, you can do so. In this particular case, Cambridge again comes top, followed this time by Newcastle, Nottingham, Oxford and York. Another indicator is the *Guardian*'s ranking according to Research Assessment. On this basis, Cardiff comes top, followed by UCL, Birmingham, Bristol and Cambridge.

2

CAREERS IN PSYCHOLOGY

There are essentially three main career routes for those who complete a degree course in psychology:

1 | To train as a professional psychologist by completing several years of further study and training at postgraduate level.
2 | To enter work or postgraduate training which builds on or relates to knowledge gained during a psychology degree programme.
3 | To find a graduate-level career which is unrelated to psychology but which may reflect your particular skills and interests.

The three routes are outlined in more detail below to give you an idea of what you might expect after three or four years of study.

1 PROFESSIONAL PSYCHOLOGY

Fewer graduates than you might expect follow this route. In order to qualify as a professional psychologist your degree course must give you the Graduate Basis for Registration (GBR) of the British Psychological Society (BPS). This is normally gained by following a course that is accredited by the Society.

Once they meet that condition, graduates will then have to start on a sometimes lengthy period of postgraduate study and practical experience to qualify for Chartered Status to enable them to practise professionally. The main professional career routes are described below.

CLINICAL PSYCHOLOGY

This is the largest specialism in professional psychology. Working mainly in the National Health Service, clinical psychologists work with clients of all ages by assessing their needs, providing therapy and carrying out research into the effects of different therapeutic methods. Their clients may be otherwise normal people who may have one of a range of problems such as drug dependency, emotional and interpersonal problems or particular learning difficulties. The clinical psychologist's role is not to be confused with that of the psychiatrist.

Entry to training programmes is highly competitive and you will need a good pass in your degree as well as relevant work experience. This can be of two kinds – either work experience in some aspect of clinical care or community work or experience as a psychology assistant working alongside existing clinical psychologists in a health authority. Vacancies for assistants occur quite frequently, but after working in this role there is no guarantee of gaining entry to a professional training programme which takes a further three years and leads to a Doctoral degree. This final stage of professional training can either take the form of full-time study at a university coupled with practical experience or an in-service training programme with a health authority.

OCCUPATIONAL PSYCHOLOGY

In comparison with other professional groups, occupational psychologists can work for a variety of employers and can be employed in a number of different roles. In government departments such as the Department for Education and Skills (DfES) and the Ministry of Defence psychologists can be involved in research or advisory work on the most effective ways of selecting, training and employing personnel. In the Disability Service they assess individual clients and advise on the kind of work and training which might suit them.

By contrast, in business consultancies, psychologists could be involved in the development of new psychological tests or in the design and delivery of company training programmes on topics such as team building. In large companies, occupational psychologists might introduce new systems for staff training and development, while in applied research they could find themselves working alongside engineers on the design of the interface between equipment and its potential user. In short, there are many potential areas of employment and freelance work. To qualify for Chartered Status in this field, psychology graduates need to complete a specialist postgraduate course lasting one year and in addition have three years' supervised work experience. Further details are available from the British Psychological Society's website.

EDUCATIONAL PSYCHOLOGY

Educational psychologists are experts in child and adolescent development. They work mainly for local education authorities and liaise with teachers and parents in identifying and assessing pupils and students with particular learning difficulties. These can range from dyslexia to disruptive classroom behaviour. Educational psychologists may not be concerned with the treatment of individual problems, but will act in a diagnostic, advisory and consultancy role. The referral of children with special educational needs to special schools is a typical example of a situation in which an educational psychologist's advice would be sought. To qualify for this specialism requires a lengthy period of further study, training and experience.

Different arrangements apply in Scotland, where educational psychologists do not need teaching experience, but in England and Wales psychology graduates are required to complete a one-year course of teacher training and have two years' teaching experience before starting a postgraduate course in Educational Psychology. This is then followed by one year of supervised practice, making it the longest qualification period of any psychology specialism.

FORENSIC PSYCHOLOGY

Often known as criminological psychologists, those in this professional group work mainly in the Prison Service, assessing prisoners in terms of their rehabilitation needs but also in terms of their level of risk. The assessment is usually based on psychometric test results and clinical interviews. In addition, forensic psychologists carry out research and put in place treatment programmes to change offending behaviour and often work with groups of offenders to achieve this aim. Some psychologists in this grouping may also appear in court proceedings to give an expert view on, for instance, the mental state of defendants.

Once again, the qualification period is three years and this comprises study for a postgraduate Master's programme, recognised by the British Psychological Society, along with supervised work experience. For details, see www.bps.org.uk/subsyst/dfp/training.cfm

HEALTH PSYCHOLOGY

Health psychologists look at the links between healthcare and illness. This can include behaviour which carries with it a health risk (such as smoking or drug use); preventative measures (exercise, diet, health checks); the delivery of healthcare; and the psychological aspects of illness, such as how patients cope with pain or terminal illness.

There are a number of accredited MSc courses for candidates who have achieved the GBR. Following this, candidates must gain two years' experience in a related field before being assessed by the BPS.

SPORTS PSYCHOLOGY

Sports psychology is a growing field. Increasingly, professional sportsmen and women are using psychologists to help them to improve their performances. Many football clubs, for instance, now employ sports psychologists to work with their players on an individual and team basis. The aim of the sports psychologist is to enhance performance by improving the focus or the motivation of the participants, and to encourage a 'will to win'.

There are no specific qualifications necessary to go into sports psychology, other than the need for a Psychology degree. Further information can be obtained from the British Association of Sport and Exercise Sciences, whose address is at the end of this book.

COUNSELLING PSYCHOLOGY

A counselling psychologist helps people to deal with problems. Typically, they might include bereavement or relationship and family problems. The counselling psychologist usually works on a one-to-one basis with the subject, and tries to help them to develop strategies to deal with life problems. To attain chartered status as a counselling psychologist, an accredited postgraduate course or a BPS diploma is required following the GBR.

Psychologists in lecturing and research

Academic staff in universities and colleges of higher education will combine teaching activities, such as delivering lectures and running seminars and tutorials, with a commitment to carry out research. Their task is to keep up to date with the latest research findings in their particular area of expertise. They will spend a considerable amount of time making applications for research funding and, once the research is completed, writing journal articles to publish their findings. Entry to academic posts in psychology is very competitive. Lecturers in higher education are not required to have a teaching qualification but those applying for lecturing posts will be expected to have a PhD and to have some published research. Lecturing posts in psychology may also arise in colleges of further education.

For psychology graduates who want to teach in schools the situation is problematic because the subject is not part of the National Curriculum. On balance it is easier for graduates to gain a place on a one-year certificate course to teach at Primary level, but even here different course centres will have their own views about whether to admit psychology graduates who will need to prove that they have the academic interests and experience to equip them for the role of primary teacher.

CASE STUDY

Peter always knew that he wanted to work with people. He enjoyed his week's work experience after GCSE at a primary school, and he decided to become a teacher. Peter took A-levels in French, sociology and history at school and gained grades BCD respectively. During his A-levels he did a variety of part-time and holiday jobs to earn some money, but the one that he found most interesting was working as a kitchen helper in a children's home. He also joined a local charity which provided helpers for summer camps for disabled children. Rather than take a teaching degree, Peter decided to study psychology at university and to get a teaching qualification afterwards. He studied a joint Psychology and Counselling degree because he liked the idea of being able to help people on a one-to-one basis. The course was weighted heavily towards psychology in the first year, but he was able to take a number of courses dealing with interpersonal relationships and communication during the course. Peter says: 'I loved the counselling parts of the course as I found that I was good at them. I found the psychology parts harder since there was quite a lot of science and even more mathematics. I would advise anyone wanting to do psychology to do some statistics before the start of the course if they haven't done A-level or AS-level maths. There is a part of the course called Research Methods which is basically A-level statistics and I really struggled with this.' Peter then took a PGCE course to train as a teacher, and now teaches psychology in a sixth form college, where he also acts as one of the college's counsellors. Next year, he is going back to university to take a postgraduate course in counselling, so that he can become a full-time counsellor.

2 RELATED CAREERS

There are several occupations for which a first degree in psychology is a useful entry qualification because of the particular knowledge or skills it provides. For example, an understanding of individual behaviour and social development is highly relevant to careers in teaching and social work. The study of statistical methods and the analysis and interpretation of statistical results can be useful in social and market research, especially when examining the results of large-scale surveys. Any insights psychology students gain into the nature of individual ability and aptitudes, and the ways these can be measured, will provide a foundation for a career in the assessment and selection of personnel. Knowledge you may acquire about physiological and cognitive psychology can be applied in ergonomics, or human factors design, as it is sometimes called. Yet again, an interest in other people's behaviour or personality may well provide the basis of careers which require an element of counselling or interpersonal helping.

By looking carefully at the content of degree programmes, the research interests of lecturing staff and specialist module options which might be available, you will soon begin to see if the course is pointing its students towards a particular career direction in applied psychology.

3 OPTIONS UNRELATED TO PSYCHOLOGY

Many graduates in psychology will choose not to apply the knowledge they have gained from their degree course, but, instead, will use the skills they have gained in a wide range of other graduate-level careers. Approximately 40 per cent of all graduate job vacancies in the UK are open to graduates irrespective of their degree subject. With a degree in psychology, therefore, it is quite possible to train as an accountant or a solicitor, enter general management, become a journalist or work in information technology. Much will depend on your particular interests and the skills you have developed.

In studying psychology students are often surprised by the number of different skills they develop and which they can use in their work after graduating:

- Information seeking and research skills - the ability to search databases and employ experimental methods.
- Analytical skills – the ability to think critically and weigh the evidence from different research findings.
- Numeracy – the ability to interpret statistical data and to assess the reliability of experimental results.
- IT skills – the ability to use software packages for data analysis and psychological measurement.

These are in addition to the skills that most higher education students will acquire such as the written communication skills developed in essay and report writing or the verbal communication skills used in group projects or seminar discussions and making presentations. As you can see, a psychology degree programme may help you to develop a broad range of skills which you can apply in the workplace, but you may need to make this apparent to potential employers.

CASE STUDY

Jessica sat A-levels in history of art, mathematics and French and gained grades BBC respectively. She was not accepted by UCL, her first choice and so she went to City University, her insurance place, to study psychology. During the course she became interested in some of the aspects of educational psychology that she studied, and decided that she wanted to look further into the problems associated with learning difficulties. She undertook some work experience at a school for children with dyslexia and was able to do some research for a book on dyslexia. At that stage she was sure that she wanted to train as an educational psychologist.

However, as part of the research for the book, Jessica visited a women's prison to talk to inmates who were dyslexic to try to find out whether people with dyslexia were disadvantaged by the legal system. As a result of this it became clear to her that law was of particular interest to her, and also that psychology as a degree was an ideal foundation for the study of law. She then went to Cambridge University to follow a one-year MSc course in Criminology and followed this with a law conversion course and the Legal Practice Course which enabled her to train as a solicitor. She now works for a large law firm in London. Jessica says: 'Although I did not end up working as a psychologist, I am very happy that I studied psychology at degree level. There are so many aspects of the course that are still useful to me now, and it allowed me to develop many skills that are important for my job as a solicitor. I really enjoyed the psychology degree course, and that was important since it made it easier to do well and I was able to get selected for the Cambridge course and for a trainee contract at a law firm. Although my A-levels were not as good as I had hoped, I was able to use the fact that I did well in my degree to go on to do the things I wanted.'

WHAT ABOUT EMPLOYABILITY?

It should be clear from the above outline of graduate opportunities that psychology is not a highly vocational degree course such as architecture or dentistry. As a subject of study it does not lead automatically to one particular kind of job. In many ways it can be seen as a semi-vocational course giving students the option of applying their subject knowledge if they choose. A key question for potential applicants to higher education courses, therefore, concerns the overall job prospects for graduates in this kind of subject. An answer is provided by the employment statistics that are collected each year by careers services. The figures below reveal the proportions of newly qualified psychology graduates in 2001, from all universities, who entered work and further study.

As you will see, over 60 per cent of psychology graduates went directly into employment and a further 21 per cent progressed to further full-time study and training – the majority undertaking postgraduate courses at Master's level.

The 'not available' category consists very largely of graduates who are taking 'time off' to travel to other countries after their degree.

Psychology graduates 2001	per cent
Entering employment	64.7
Going on to further study	20.9
Not available for work, etc	7.9
Believed unemployed	5.6
Seeking work or further study but not unemployed	1.0

Of those in the survey who went directly into employment, about 17 per cent gained jobs which were business or finance related, whilst others found employment in healthcare (14 per cent), retail (9 per cent), marketing and the media (5 per cent), and teaching (4 per cent).

Source: *What Do Graduates Do?* 2002. Produced by CSU, AGCAS, UCAS and HESA.

3

APPLICATIONS: SECTION 10 OF THE UCAS FORM

For general advice on completing your UCAS form, see another book in this series: *How to Complete Your UCAS Form*.

This chapter is designed to help you plan Section 10: your personal statement. This is the only chance you get to prove that, on paper, you deserve a place, or at least an interview, at the universities of your choice. It's vital that you think very carefully about what to say in order to show yourself in the best possible light. It may sound obvious, but they only know what you tell them.

The content of Section 10 is unique to each candidate. There are no rules, as such, but there are recommendations that can be made.

Universities are primarily academic institutions so you must present yourself as a strong bet. The first thing that the admissions tutor wants to know is the strength of your commitment to study. Say clearly why you wish to study for your chosen degree, especially if you haven't studied psychology before. Wanting to work with people, or liking children, is not good enough. Give details of particular areas of study that interest you and say what you hope to get out of researching them at university level. Bookshops have sections on 'popular psychology' which contain books about psychology for non-psychologists – this is a good starting point if you wish to demonstrate an interest in the subject but haven't studied it at AS or A-level. A word of warning: don't try to impress the selectors by claiming that you have read degree-level psychology books as you may get asked about your reading if you are called for interview – stick to things that you can understand and discuss. A selection of some popular titles is listed at the end of the book in the section on psychology texts.

If there have been certain bits of your AS or A-level psychology course which you have enjoyed, say so and tell them why. If you are new to the subject, give examples from newspapers, television events or controversies that have appealed to the psychologist in you. Give examples of your academic interest and explain your reasons for them.

Work experience is useful as it demonstrates a commitment to the subject outside the classroom. If you have had relevant work experience, talk about it on your form. Explain concisely what your job entailed, for example:

'During the summer vacation, I am a volunteer at a summer camp for children with learning disabilities. This has been a most valuable work experience and I thoroughly enjoyed working with the children. I have also developed good teamwork and communication skills and have even learnt some sign language!'

Future plans can also be included, if you have them. Again, be precise and informative. This will demonstrate a breadth of interest in the subject.

At least half of Section 10 should deal with material directly related to your chosen course. Thereafter, use the rest of the page to tell the admissions tutor what makes you who you are. What travel have you undertaken? What music do you like and/or play? What do you read? What sporting achievements do you have? In all these things give details.

'Last year I went to France. I like reading and listening to music and sometimes I play football at weekends' is weak. A stronger version might read:

'Last year I drove through France and enjoyed visiting the chateaux of the Loire. I relax by reading the novels of Stephen King and have hardback

first editions of all his books. My musical taste is extremely wide, ranging from Gregorian Chant to Robbie Williams and I would like to continue playing the cello in an orchestra at university. I would also be keen to play in a football team to keep myself fit.'

Don't expect to fit everything about yourself on this single page and only write things that you are prepared to expand on at interview. The idea is to whet their appetite and to make them want to meet you.

4

SUCCEEDING IN YOUR INTERVIEW

Depending on where you apply, you may not get called for interview at all since only a few of the universities now conduct formal interviews. However, a number of universities – usually those with the highest ratio of applicants per place – still ask students to attend a formal interview, and others combine open days with more informal meetings. If you do apply to a university that interviews applicants, don't worry: the interview is a chance for you to demonstrate to the selectors your suitability for the course. It will not be an unpleasant experience as long as you do your preparation.

GENERAL HINTS FOR INTERVIEWS

■ While the number of people conducting the interview and the length of time it takes can vary, all interviews are designed to enable those asking the questions to find out as much about the candidate as they can. It is important, therefore, to engage actively with the process (good eye contact and confident body language help) and treat it as a chance to put yourself across rather than as an obstacle course trying to catch you out.

- Interviewers are more interested in what you know than in what you don't know. If you are asked something you can't answer, say so. To waffle (or worse, to lie) simply wastes time and lets you down. The interviewers will be considering the quality of thought that goes into your answers; they will not expect you to know everything already. Pauses while you think are perfectly acceptable; don't be afraid to take your time.
- It is likely that one, or more, of the interviewers will be your tutor(s) during your time at university. Enthusiasm for, a strong commitment to, and a willingness to learn your chosen subject are all extremely important attitudes to convey. The people you meet at interview not only have to judge your academic calibre, but also have to decide whether they would enjoy teaching you for the next three to four years. Try to demonstrate your enthusiasm by mentioning books or articles that you have read, or topics that you enjoyed as part of your AS- or A-level psychology course.
- An ability to think on your feet is vital. Pre-learned responses never work: they appear glib and superficial and, no matter how apparently spontaneously they are delivered, they are always detectable. Putting forward an answer step by step, using examples and factual knowledge to reinforce your points, is far more professional, even if you are not completely sure of what you are saying. That said, it is also sensible to admit defeat: knowing you are beaten is a more intelligent thing than mindlessly clinging to the wreckage of a specious case.
- It is possible to steer the interview yourself to some extent. If, for example, you are asked to comment on something you know little about, confidently replacing the question with another related one shows enthusiasm. Don't waste time in silences that are as embarrassing for the panel as for the candidate.
- Essential preparation includes revision of the personal section of your UCAS form. This may well form the basis of preliminary questions (which are meant to put you at your ease) and if it proves to be a mass of fabrications, the interview is doomed from the start!
- Questions may well be asked about your extracurricular activities. Again, this is to put you at your ease: your answers should be thorough and enthusiastic, but not too long!
- At the end of the interview you are normally given a chance to ask questions of your own. If you have none, say that the

interview has covered all the queries you had. It is sensible, though, to have one or two questions of a serious kind – about the course, the tuition, etc – up your sleeve. Don't ask anything that you could, and should, have found answers to in the prospectus. It is also fine, even desirable, to base a question on the interview itself. This marks you out as someone who listens, is curious and who is keen to learn.

■ Above all, make them remember you when they go through a list of 20 or more applicants at the end of the day.

CASE STUDY

Natasha studied A-levels in chemistry, biology and mathematics at a boarding school in Surrey. She ended up with two A grades and a B. She was offered places to study psychology at UCL and Edinburgh and had a hard time trying to decide which one to accept. 'In the end, it came down to accommodation – my brother had a flat in London where I could stay and this made the choice easier.' The course was demanding: 'There was a heavy work load and the lecturers and tutors expected us to spend many hours in the library or on the internet researching things and looking beyond the lecture notes. I found this hard at first, but began to see that this was a much more satisfying way to work than A-level where we simply had to remember lots of facts to do well.'

'I don't know why I actually decided to study psychology initially – I think that it sounded interesting. My first university interview was a disaster! I was asked why I wanted to study psychology and I said lots of very stupid things about being interested in the way people relate to each other. I was rejected, and so I knew that I had to do some research. I read lots of books and as well as being much better prepared for the interview, I actually realised that I really did want to study psychology.'

FINDING THE FACTS

Although admissions interviews are not offered routinely by all universities, staff will try to ensure that applicants have a chance to visit the course centre to find out more about the learning environment. Some, for example, will offer group interviews in which a member of staff will lead a discussion about the degree programme, enabling applicants to ask questions about the course. Others will host open days and campus tours which provide applicants with the chance of talking to current students about the 'student experience' and viewing the university's facilities.

You should take every opportunity to visit the higher education institutions to which you are applying because, in themselves, prospectus entries will only give you part of the picture. The checklist below will give you an idea of the kinds of questions to ask when you visit a university or college to find out more about a particular course.

QUESTIONS YOU NEED TO ASK

1 | About entry

- What additional information is available about the course of study, apart from that in the prospectus?
- What are the aims and objectives of the course?
- What size is the first year intake?
- What entry grades are required? How strictly are these kept to?

2 | About study and learning

- Apart from courses in psychology, what other ancillary courses will I need to take?
- What are the class-contact hours for first year students?
- How much time will I have for private study?
- What are the main teaching activities?
- Over the duration of the programme, what proportion of my time will I spend in lectures, seminars, practicals, project work and placements ?
- Will it help if I have my own personal computer?

3 | About assessment and learning support

- Will I have a personal tutor?
- Are there specific courses in study methods?
- How will my work be assessed?
- Will my first year results count towards the final degree result?

■ Are there opportunities to have coaching/mentoring from more experienced students?

■ What happens if students fail their first year?

4| About career opportunities and employment

■ Do present students receive help in finding part-time work to help pay for the cost of accommodation, fees, etc?

■ Is the course recognised by the British Psychology Society, giving the Graduate Basis for Registration?

■ Where does the degree course lead in terms of career opportunities and further study?

■ What links do lecturers have with employers and practising professional psychologists?

■ Are there particular course modules designed to help students with their career decisions?

These questions are largely concerned with the student experience from the perspective of academic study. Intending students are, in addition, likely to have a range of other questions concerning accommodation, finance and the kind of facilities each university has to offer.

5

THE UNIVERSITIES AND COLLEGES: COURSE DETAILS

Use this section to read a bit more about each of the places on your shortlist. They are arranged alphabetically and each one gives a contact address. The information has been provided by the universities.

You should always check the university websites and prospectuses before making an application, as the courses available, course content, and entrance requirements may change.

ABERDEEN UNIVERSITY

The University of Aberdeen, Regents Walk, Aberdeen AB24 3FX
Tel: 01224 272090

Aberdeen offers Psychology as a single Honours degree under both BSc and MA degree schemes. It can also be studied as combined Honours with a modern language, and as a joint Honours with Computing Science, Anthropology, Philosophy, Sociology or Statistics. The Scottish degree structure provides breadth and flexibility in the early stages, so that the final choice of degree does not have to be made until the end of the second year. Progress to junior Honours (level 3) is dependent on good performance in the levels 1 and 2 Psychology assessments. The level 3 curriculum includes courses on methodology, biopsychology, perception, development psychology, human memory and social psychology. In level 4 students have a choice of options, and carry out and report on an empirical investigation. Students can apply to study abroad for part of their degree under European or North American exchange programmes. The Honours degrees are accredited by the BPS.

ABERTAY DUNDEE UNIVERSITY

University of Abertay Dundee, Bell Street, Dundee DD1 1HG
Tel: 01382 308080

BSc Behavioural Sciences involves the integrated study of psychology and sociology, strongly focusing on human motivation, behaviour and thought processes. The course is designed to ensure you develop an understanding of both subjects and their impact on each other. Practical problem solving and the gathering and analysis of data are emphasised. If your performance reaches the standard required by the BPS, you may opt to specialise in psychology in year three and exit after year four with an accredited BSc degree in Psychology. There is a wide range of options in the final year, including cognitive, social, health and clinical psychology, neuropsychology, criminal behaviour and counselling. BSc (Hons) Forensic Psychobiology is a BPS accredited programme covering core areas of Psychology whilst enabling students to specialise in forensic topics. All final year students submit a supervised project in an area of special interest to them

ASTON

Aston University, Aston Triangle, Birmingham B4 7ET
Tel: 0121 359 3611

You can choose between three-year and four-year sandwich BSc Human Psychology degree programmes, both conferring eligibility for graduate membership of the BPS, essential for a professional career in psychology. The four-year sandwich programme includes a twelve-month professional work placement between year two and the final year. Over half of Aston Psychology graduates take a placement year and it is especially recommended for those seeking a professional career in psychology, in clinical psychology for example. Students can switch between the three- and four-year programmes so a final decision about whether or not to take a placement need not be taken at application. (Apply for either the three- or the four-year programme.) There is also a foundation year programme available only to mature students who have not recently sat A-levels. Psychology can be taken as 50 per cent of a combined Honours degree in combination with a wide range of subjects. Combinations with biology, sociology, a language and business are popular but combined degrees do not confer eligibility for graduate membership of the BPS. There is a wide range of final-year options enabling students to tailor their studies to fit their own interests and career path. Aston emphasises the human and the applied aspects of psychology and graduate employability. Aston Psychology teaching is officially rated as excellent and the department has a strong record (grade 5) especially in neuroscience. As the Human Psychology degree gives you a grounding in the human and social sciences, familiarity with carrying out and evaluating research and the statistical treatment of data, a high degree of literacy and an ability to argue a case (psychology is never a cut and dried subject), graduates are able to go on to a very wide range of careers in addition to professional psychology.

BATH SPA UNIVERSITY COLLEGE

Bath Spa University College, Newton Park, Bath BA2 9BN
Tel: 01225 875875

Bath Spa offers Psychology as a BA/BSc such as neuropsychology and evolutionary psychology in combined programmes. It offers a wide range of optional modules allowing psychology specialists to develop their interests and non-specialists to complement their studies. The course is not BPS approved.

BATH UNIVERSITY

The University of Bath, Claverton Down, Bath BA2 7AY
Tel: 01225 826826

Bath provides a four-year sandwich course in Psychology, giving a grounding across the discipline, with a particular focus on social, health, developmental and cognitive psychology. Students will also be expected to take courses from the following options: social and policy science, a modern language or biology. Final year options can be all psychology or a combination from the above options. These are taught by staff who are actively researching in these areas. Examples currently include economic and political psychology, health and clinical psychology, artificial intelligence, controversies in cognition and post-modern psychology. Assessment is approximately 50 per cent coursework and 50 per cent examination in the overall degree. The department emphasises the importance of training students in marketable and transferable skills, and students are required to spend their third year on placement (this may be unpaid) in one of a wide range of settings within professional psychology, including clinical, educational, occupational or research settings, both home or overseas. Most final year dissertations arise out of research work done during the placement. Students find the placement year invaluable as a preparation for career choice. BSc in Psychology and Communications Engineering is also offered.

BELFAST, QUEEN'S UNIVERSITY

Queen's University of Belfast, University Road, Belfast, Northern Ireland BT7 1NN
Tel: 028 902 45133

The 1999 subject review of psychology rated the teaching quality of Psychology at Queen's as 'excellent', awarding a maximum score of 24. Students follow a three-year degree programme leading to an Honours degree in Psychology (accredited by the BPS). The school has extensive computing facilities for students. It has specialised teaching facilities for cognitive, perception, social, developmental, psychobiology, sport and exercise psychology, and animal behaviour. The school has close links with local hospitals and schools where many students undertake projects. The school offers opportunities to study a wide variety of topics covering the breadth of the discipline.

For more information see www.psych.qub.ac.uk

BIRMINGHAM UNIVERSITY	The University of Birmingham, Edgbaston, Birmingham B15 2TT Tel: 0121 414 3344

Birmingham's School of Psychology is a large psychology department with a top research rating of 5* and an 'excellent' rating of teaching and learning of 23/24. The school has close relationships with local hospitals, clinics, schools, industrial companies and departments of local and national government. The single Honours BSc degree is structured so that for the first two years students follow a common programme in the core areas of psychology, while the final year allows some specialisation in areas of interest

BOLTON INSTITUTE	Bolton Institute, Dean Road, Bolton BL3 5AB Tel: 01204 903903

The Psychology course is the largest single pathway within the Institute and currently has some 388 students. Psychology may be studied in single, joint, major or minor modes; however, only the single, joint and major modes grant eligibility for graduate membership of the British Psychological Society and gives graduates a basis for registration. The modular degree scheme offers students both mandatory and optional modules. Students study six modules each year (three per semester), which cover all aspects of psychology. In the final year each student conducts an individual research project as well as studying specialised modules. Teaching and research accommodation includes lecture theatres, laboratories, computer suites and a video laboratory.

BOURNEMOUTH UNIVERSITY	Bournemouth University, Studland House, 12 Christchurch Road, Bournemouth, Dorset BH1 3NA Tel: 01202 524111

It is important today that those who are essentially interested in human behaviour know something about technological systems – how they can be used to help people, and how their design can be improved to this end. People of a more technological inclination need to know something about the people who will use or otherwise be affected by their designs. The three-year BSc Applied

Psychology and Computing course examines the interaction of psychological and computing factors in the development of effective, safe and satisfying computer systems.

BRADFORD UNIVERSITY

University of Bradford, Bradford, West Yorkshire BD7 1DP
Tel: 01274 232323

Bradford offers a BA (Honours) in Interdisciplinary Human Studies which enables you to combine psychology, sociology, philosophy, literature and communication studies. This gives you a broad knowledge of human studies. The course was launched in 1973 and has twice received national commendation. The first two years provide you with the foundations of all the disciplines. In the final year, you may pursue your own interests in greater depth by focusing on one discipline or bringing an interdisciplinary approach to a particular course.

BRISTOL UNIVERSITY

University of Bristol, Senate House, Bristol BS8 1TH
Tel: 0117 928 9000

The Bristol Psychology Department has active links with other departments including child health and sport, exercise and health sciences and with the Burden Neurological Institute. Bristol offers a BSc in Experimental Psychology in the Sciences and joint Honours degrees in Psychology with Zoology or Philosophy. In the final year, students are encouraged to present reports of projects at an annual South West Area Student Conference.

BRISTOL, UNIVERSITY OF WEST ENGLAND

University of the West of England, Faculty of Applied Sciences (Psychology), Frenchay Campus, Coldharbour Lane, Bristol BS16 1QY
Tel: 0117 328 3333 (Enquiry and Admissions Service)

UWE offers BSc (Hons) Psychology; Psychology with Health Science; Psychology and Forensic Science. Psychology is also available as a joint Honours option. Most degrees can be studied full time or part time. BSc (Hons) Psychology and Psychology with Health Science have been designed to give a thorough understanding of psychology and its applications, and the Psychology with Health Science course particularly looks at the relationship to health and healthcare.

BRUNEL UNIVERSITY

Brunel University, Uxbridge, Middlesex UB8 3PH
Tel: 01895 274000

There are possibilities to study for either a BSc in Psychology or a BSc joint Honours combining Psychology with Sociology or Social Anthropology. The early stage of the course involves a multidisciplinary approach which is followed by opportunities to specialise. Teaching is heavily influenced by research interests of the staff. The thin sandwich degree is designed to link academic theory with work experience gained over two separate placements. Students may enter the caring professions, commercial organisations or a public sector organisation. The department helps find suitable placements and some are paid. However, students are encouraged to pursue their own placements, particularly if they would like to go abroad.

BUCKINGHAM UNIVERSITY

University of Buckingham, Hunter Street, Buckingham MK18 1EG
Tel: 01280 814080

The Department of Psychology at Buckingham offers Psychology either as a single honours BSc course or combined with a minor subject. Minor options are Business Studies, Marketing, Information Systems, Media Communications, English Literature, Socio-Legal Studies, French, Spanish and English Language Studies (for non-native speakers only). All psychology degrees are two years' duration starting in January and with four terms per year. The department accepts many mature and overseas students. Courses are not currently BPS accredited but Buckingham graduates have successfully obtained BPS GBR through conversion courses or the BPS in-house exams.

BUCKING-
HAMSHIRE
CHILTERNS
UNIVERSITY
COLLEGE

Buckinghamshire Chilterns University College, High Wycombe Campus, Queen Alexandra Road, High Wycombe, Buckinghamshire HP11 2IZ
Tel: 01494 522141

Courses at Buckinghamshire Chilterns are structured on a modular basis over two semesters per year. Students study four modules per semester. Psychology can be studied as either single Honours (BSc (Hons) Psychology) or in combination with the following subjects: Sociology, Criminology, Computing and Sports. Additionally, a BSc (Hons) in Criminological Psychology is now offered. The BSc (Hons) Psychology is recognised by the BPS and confers the GBR. Psychology is located in a purpose built building with specialist facilities for laboratory work in areas of practical psychology.

CAMBRIDGE
UNIVERSITY

Cambridge Admissions Office, Kellet Lodge, Tennis Court Road, Cambridge CB2 1QJ
Tel: 01223 333308

Psychology is part of a BA in Natural Sciences or the BA in Social and Political Sciences. The natural sciences course is based on general scientific training and allows you to study experimental psychology along with other scientific subjects and to specialise in it in the final year. There is the opportunity to work with leading scientists and within the Medical Research Council's Cognition and Brain Sciences Unit, a leading laboratory in psychology research. Competition for places is tough! Psychology is one option within the Social and Political Sciences course. Psychology is studied within Politics and Sociology. Those who take the requisite scheme of study in Psychology are normally eligible for admission to professional courses in clinical and educational psychology through graduate membership of the BPS.

CANTERBURY
CHRIST
CHURCH
UNIVERSITY
COLLEGE

Canterbury Christ Church University College, North Holmes Road, Canterbury, Kent CT1 1QU
Tel: 01227 782900

Psychology is offered within the Department of Applied Social Sciences as a combined degree (BA/BSc), and is available as a major, joint or minor programme. The Psychology programme provides compulsory introductory courses in the first year, and options in years two and three. Courses aim to provide students with a sound discipline as well as equipping them with a wide range of transferable skills. The programme considers students from a variety of academic backgrounds including Access courses, AVCE and A-level. It is not, however, recognised by the BPS.

CARDIFF UNIVERSITY

Cardiff University, PO Box 901, Cardiff CF11 3YG
Tel: 029 2087 4404

The School of Psychology, one of the largest in Britain, has recently been commended in independent assessments for the quality of its research and teaching. The school offers four single (recognised by the BPS for Graduate Membership and GBR) and three joint Honours undergraduate degrees. Psychology (three year) and Applied Psychology (four-year sandwich) are offered as BA or BSc courses. The joint Psychology/Education degree is also recognised by the BPS. Joint Honours degrees combine Psychology with Criminology, Education or Physiology. Teaching includes formal lectures combined with practical classes, computer workshops, video demonstrations and small group tutorial work. Students receive a sound foundation in psychology with the opportunity to focus on their own interests in the final year. Excellent computing and laboratory facilities support the teaching and staff research activities which include family relationships, virtual reality, fault-finding in industry, neuropsychology, the effects of drugs on behaviour, motion perception, face recognition and health psychology.

CENTRAL LANCASHIRE UNIVERSITY

University of Central Lancashire, Preston PR1 2HE
Tel: 01772 201201

There are two routes through the course leading to either a BSc in Psychology or a BSc in Applied Psychology. Initially students take the same modules and as long as you take the 'Introduction to Applied Psychology' module in the second year, you can delay the decision of which course to follow to the end of that year. Psychology may be studied as a major, joint or minor subject on the combined Honours programme which allows for flexibility. You can study a language as an option and take part in study opportunities abroad.

UNIVERSITY COLLEGE CHESTER

University College Chester, Parkgate Road, Chester CH1 4BJ
Tel: 01244 375444

Chester offers Psychology in single and combined Honours degrees, the latter with a wide range of subject combinations in both Arts and Humanities and Science and Health. The degrees are modular and particular routes in single and combined Honours degrees bring eligibility for GBR with the BPS. Core modules are completed in five semesters and the final semester offers a wide choice of optional modules. Stress is placed on practical work and research methods and many modules have an applied slant, ie looking at the contribution of psychology to real world problems, eg educational, organisational and forensic psychology.

CITY UNIVERSITY

City University, Northampton Square, London EC1V 0HB
Tel: 020 7040 5060

The Department of Psychology, which is within the School of Social Sciences, offers a single Honours degree in Psychology. Psychology does not contribute to any joint Honours degrees within the School. In the first year students take introductory courses in a range of areas in psychology, as well as one elective module from outside psychology. The second year provides a thorough grounding in the principal areas of psychology, and the third year offers a range of elective modules from both theoretical and applied areas of psychology. The degree qualifies students for membership of the BPS and for Graduate Basis for Registration of the BPS, required for the pursuit of professional training in psychology.

COVENTRY UNIVERSITY

Coventry University, Priory Street, Coventry CV1 5FB
Tel: 024 7688 7688

Psychology at Coventry University covers a broad and exciting range of specialist and applied areas, which include forensic psychology, health psychology, clinical psychology (all of which are taught at postgraduate level) as well as parapsychology, transpersonal psychology, organisational psychology and media psychology. The university manages three degrees all of which confer eligibility for the Graduate Basis of Registration with the BPS. There are:

BSc (Hons) Psychology
BSc (Hons) Psychology and Criminology
BSc (Hons) Psychology and Sociology

A student-centred approach to learning is supported by a strong system of personal tutorials. You will also develop a range of transferable skills that are attractive to employers. The provision of psychology is also fully supported by WebCT – an online learning environment.

CREWE & ALSAGER CHE

See Manchester Metropolitan University.

DE MONTFORT UNIVERSITY

De Montfort University, The Gateway, Leicester LE1 9BH
Tel: 0116 255 1551

De Montfort University offers a BSc (Honours) in Human Psychology as well as joint Honours degrees in Psychology. The aim of the Human Psychology single Honours programme is to provide students with an insight into the human mind, human abilities and human behaviour. The joint Honours degrees offer students programmes combining psychology with other subjects. The Psychology syllabus covers areas such as cultural psychology, counselling psychology, criminological and forensic psychology, emotion, sexuality and gender. Assessment methods vary from 'email essays', multiple-choice exams, and practical work to the traditional essay and exam formats.

DERBY UNIVERSITY

University of Derby, Kedleston Road, Derby DE22 1GB
Tel: 01332 622222

Derby offers a BSc Psychology degree, a BSc in Psychology and Counselling Studies, and psychology pathways within the university's combined subjects programme. All can be taken full or part time and the BSc Psychology degree is also available as an online course. Students who graduate from the two specialist programmes obtain the Graduate Basis for Registration with the BPS, as do those majoring in Psychology within the combined subjects programme. Also offered is a BSc in Psychological Studies, which does not provide BPS recognition but allows students grater choice and flexibility in their programme of study. Courses are offered on a modular basis and a variety of assessment methods are used, matched to the content of individual modules. Psychology teaching covers the main theories and methods of contemporary psychology. Many modules include some practical work.

DUNDEE UNIVERSITY

The University, Dundee DD1 4HN
Tel: 01382 223181

Psychology may be taken in the Faculty of Arts and Social Sciences or the Faculty of Science, Faculty of Life Sciences or Faculty of Engineering and Physical Sciences. Most psychology teaching is devoted to courses leading to Honours degrees (four years) and general degrees (three years). The course reflects the research interests of the teaching staff but there is an overriding commitment to present a balanced view of the subject. Laboratory work and experience with computers form an integral part of the practical training.

DURHAM UNIVERSITY

University of Durham, Department of Psychology, Science Laboratories, South Road, Durham DH1 3LE
Tel: 0191 334 3240

The Department of Psychology offers single Honours degrees in Psychology as well as participating in Natural Science, combined Honours and joint Honours degrees. The department also offers a BSc Honours degree in Applied Psychology at its Stockton campus. The courses cover a broad range of topics from biological psychology to social psychology. Members of staff are active in all research fields of psychology, with strengths in cognitive psychology, developmental psychology and neuroscience.

EAST LONDON UNIVERSITY

University of East London, Romford Road, London E15 4LZ
Tel: 020 8590 7722

Available full time and part time and in both the day and evening, the BSc course (BPS accredited) offers a wide choice of specialist study including: psychology of mental health, cognitive neuropsychology, drugs and behaviour, counselling, developing minds, animal behaviour, occupational, evolutionary and forensic psychology. The department also offers postgraduate research courses in all the main areas of professional applied psychology as well as having numerous postgraduate research students. A graduate Diploma course is also offered for graduates of other disciplines who wish to convert their first degree to one which is acceptable for registration with the BPS.

EDGE HILL

Edge Hill, St Helens Road, Ormskirk, Lancs L39 4QP
Tel: 01695 575171

The course leads to a BSc single Honours degree in Psychology (with BPS GBR). The three-year full-time programme covers all of the major areas that feature in the BPS qualifying examination: cognitive psychology; social psychology; developmental psychology; biological psychology; personality and individual differences and research methods. In the third year a number of specialist options are available including work psychology, educational psychology, addiction studies, mental health, and the psychology of personal relationships. Students also undertake a supervised research project in their final year. Psychology was rated 'excellent' for its teaching by HEFCE in its most recent inspection. The course is taught in new purpose-built psychology laboratories. A range of facilities is available including Internet and CD-ROM systems, for example, online journals and abstract databases.

EDINBURGH UNIVERSITY

The University of Edinburgh, Old College, South Bridge, Edinburgh EH8 9YL
Tel: 0131 650 1000

Single Honours degrees (four years) are available in the Faculty of Social Sciences and in the Faculty of Science and Engineering. There are several joint Honours degrees in which psychology is studied to Honours level along with another subject: artificial intelligence, business studies, linguistics, philosophy or sociology. In the first three years, all students study a broad range of psychological topics representing the core areas of the discipline. In the fourth year, students can specialise by choosing from a wide variety of options linked to the research expertise of individual members of staff.

ESSEX UNIVERSITY

University of Essex, Wivenhoe Park, Colchester C04 3SQ
Tel: 01206 873666

Psychology is offered both as a BA and a BSc which builds on the university's strengths in cognitive science, linguistics and social sciences. The course covers the biological basis of behaviour, language, memory, perception, individual differences and child development. These are BPS accredited schemes. From 2004 the university will also offer specialist degrees in Developmental Psychology (BPS accreditation pending). Finally the Department of Health and Human Sciences runs two degree schemes which may be of interest – BSc Social Psychology and Sociology, and the BSc in Health Psychology and Health Science. Neither are BPS accredited schemes.

EXETER UNIVERSITY

University of Exeter, Northcote House, The Queen's Drive, Exeter EX4 4QJ
Tel: 01392 263035

The programme may be a BSc or a BA; the main syllabus is the same. Exeter also offers an interdepartmental single Honours BSc in Cognitive Science which works in collaboration with Computer Science. The emphasis is on computational models of mental processes and the study of language, thought and skills. The School of Psychology achieved 'excellent', 23 out of 24 in the QAA exercise and grade 8 in the RAE, recognising excellent research internationally. Selection for non-mature applicants is based mainly on A-level performance and the overall UCAS application form.

GLAMORGAN UNIVERSITY	University of Glamorgan, Pontypridd CF37 1DL Tel: 01443 480480

A single Honours BSc is on offer which leads to GBR with the BPS, or as a BA joint Honours degree, combining Psychology with a wide range of possible subjects. Glamorgan also offers major/minor routes in psychology. It has good links with sports science and also offers a degree in Sports Psychology.

GLASGOW UNIVERSITY	University of Glasgow, Glasgow G12 8QQ Tel: 0141 330 6062

Psychology is offered in the faculties of Arts (MA), Science (BSc) and Social Sciences (MA SocSci), the faculty being determined by the subjects you wish to combine with psychology. The faculty you enter affects the subjects you will study alongside psychology in the first two years of the course. The Honours course is taken over four years and can either be single Honours or joint Honours with a variety of combinations possible. The single Honours and joint Honours degrees are both approved as conferring eligibility for graduate membership of the BPS. All core areas of psychology are covered, together with statistics and experimental design as well as other topic areas which reflect the expertise and research areas of the staff. In the final year students carry out an independent research project. The department has a strong research record in various areas, eg perception, neuroscience, addictions, language and cognitive science. In the recent Teaching Quality Assurance Assessment the department received an 'excellent' and the last Research Assessment Exercise awarded the department the elite 5* rating.

GLASGOW CALEDONIAN UNIVERSITY	Glasgow Caledonian University, Cowcaddens Road, Glasgow G4 0BA Tel: 0141 331 3000

The BSc/BSc (Hons) Psychology programme provides a rewarding and challenging undergraduate education in psychology while allowing students to select modules from complementary non-psychology subject areas.

In years 1 and 2, the study of psychology is balanced with options chosen from a range of designated subject areas including sociology, politics, history, economics, marketing, media studies, biology, chemistry, physics, mathematics, environmental studies and European languages. In years 3 and 4, students can specialise entirely in psychology or continue to study another subject area if they wish to do so.

All students who successfully complete each level of the programme are eligible to proceed to Honours if they wish, without further selection. The Honours programme is recognised by the British Psychological Society as meeting their Graduate Basis for Registration (GBR).

GLOUCESTER-SHIRE UNIVERSITY

School of Health and Social Sciences, University of Gloucestershire, Francis Close Hall, Swindon Road, Cheltenham, Gloucestershire GL50 4AZ
Tel: 01242 536197

Psychology is available as a BSc or BA in a major/joint/minor structure, combining with a wide range of subjects including sociology, sports science, business management, English and media communications. The course offers full coverage of the BPS syllabus, and for major students is recognised for Graduate Membership and GBR. A particular strength of the course is its coverage of topics in applied psychology and critical psychology.

GREENWICH UNIVERSITY

University of Greenwich, The School of Health and Social Care, Avery Hill Campus, Avery Hill Road, London SE9 2UG
Tel: 020 8331 8928

Psychology students receive training which allows them to work as professional psychologists and as generalist graduates in a range of occupations. The BSc (Hons) Psychology is approved as conferring eligibility for Graduate Membership of the BPS. The BSc in Psychology begins with introductory 30 credit units in research methods, individual differences, developmental and social psychology, and cognitive behavioural neuroscience. All students undertake laboratory work including working with computers using the SPSS statistical package.

HERTFORDSHIRE UNIVERSITY

University of Hertfordshire, College Lane, Hatfield, Hertfordshire AL10 9AB
Tel: 01707 284000

The first year of the BSc Honours Psychology lays a strong foundation in core areas of empirical psychology. Modules in applied developmental and social psychology in the second year underpin a choice of final-year option courses. In the final year, students carry out an independent research project under the supervision of an experienced researcher. There is an optional short work placement. The BSc (Hons) Cognitive Science and the BSc (Hons) Psychology with Artificial Intelligence degrees offer students the opportunity to study psychology, computer programming, philosophy, linguistics and neuroscience in an integrated programme that addresses questions of human and machine intelligence. The BSc Psychology and the BSc Psychology with AI both hold BPS accreditation.

HUDDERSFIELD UNIVERSITY

University of Huddersfield, Queensgate, Huddersfield HD1 3DH
Tel: 01484 422288

The first year of the BSc (Hons) in Psychology comprises introductory modules in psychology, sociology and research methods. The second year builds upon the first year with more advanced modules, while in the third and final year students have the opportunity to take specialist modules in psychology and other areas of behavioural sciences. The degree is accredited by the British Psychological Society giving students the Graduate Basis for Registration. The BSc (Hons) in Social Psychology shares some modules with the BSc (Hons) in Psychology but approaches the discipline from a more social perspective. The BSc (Hons) in Psychology and Computing provides students with the skills and knowledge to work in a computing profession that demands an understanding of human needs and contributions in technology.

HULL
UNIVERSITY

University of Hull, Hull HU6 7RX
Tel: 01482 465388

This is a three-year BSc in Psychology that is hierarchically organised into levels arranged so that in the first year you will receive a broad introduction to psychology and in subsequent years modules become more specialised and advanced. Hull also offers a four-year Psychology with Occupational Psychology, a three-year Psychology with Counselling Psychology, and joint Honours degrees combining psychology with sociology, anthropology, philosophy, criminology or sports science. These joint courses last for three years and students spend approximately 70 per cent of their study on psychology components and 30 per cent on their other subject. There is also direct entry to postgraduate clinical psychology training from the psychology courses. All courses are accredited by the BPS for graduate registration.

KEELE
UNIVERSITY

The University, Keele, Staffordshire ST5 5BG
Tel: 01782 621111

Students combine psychology with another subject following a dual Honours degree programme which leads to accreditation by the British Psychological Society. In addition, first-year students take a one-year course in Complementary Studies which is designed to introduce a third discipline area and develop their academic skills. Over thirty combinations are available with psychology in a dual Honours programme which include disciplines from the Humanities, the Social Sciences and the Natural Sciences. Criminology is the most popular subject followed by English, biology, sociology and neuroscience. A modular scheme is followed in which all students take two psychology modules per semester. Students can spend a semester at one of Keele's North American partner institutions during their second year. The department has particular strengths in social psychology and social development, cognition and cognitive development, health psychology and music psychology.

KENT UNIVERSITY

University of Kent at Canterbury, Kent CT2 7NZ
Tel: 01227 764000

Kent offers degrees in Psychology, Social Psychology, Social Psychology with Clinical Psychology, Applied Psychology, Applied Social Psychology with Clinical Psychology, Psychology with Law and European Social Psychology. There is the opportunity to spend a year at a European university under the Psychology and European Social Psychology courses. Four-year degrees include a placement where students undertake special project work in the NHS, Prison Service or a government research establishment. In the final year students are able to choose from a wide range of specialist options including options in cognitive, developmental, forensic, health and social psychology.

KING ALFRED'S CHE

King Alfred's College, Sparkford Road, Winchester, Hampshire SO22 4NR
Tel: 01962 841515

This is an accredited college of Southampton University but applications are made directly to the college. Psychology is offered as a single Honours programme or as part of a combined Honours programme in which you take two subjects. After the first year in which all students study two subjects, you may choose to study psychology as single Honours, or as a main, equal or minor part of your degree. The single Honours and main (75 per cent) pathway in psychology are accredited by the BPS with GBR. The psychology department has good community links (eg NHS links, schools, etc) both in Winchester and within Hampshire, and national and international research links. This is a small, friendly department with a strong emphasis on learning and teaching.

KINGSTON UNIVERSITY

Kingston University, Penrhyn Road, Kingston upon Thames, Surrey KT1 2EE
Tel: 020 8547 2000

Psychology is offered under a modular framework giving students considerable autonomy. Tutors are drawn from different faculties. The full BSc Honours degree in Psychology and the major psychology route are now accredited by BPS and the half field route confers GBR on the student.

LANCASTER UNIVERSITY

Lancaster University, University House, Lancaster LA1 4YW
Tel: 01524 593698

People typically register for a BA or a BSc on the basis of what minor subjects they want to do. You take three subjects in your first year and then concentrate on psychology in the second and third year. There is also a variety of combined degrees. Those combining psychology with a foreign language do a four-year course with one year spent abroad. You can choose whether to graduate with a BA or a BSc.

Specific combined degrees include Psychology and Organisation Studies, Educational Studies, Linguistics or Women's Studies.

LA SAINTE UNION CHE

La Sainte Union College, The Avenue, Southampton, Hampshire
SO9 5HB
Tel: 023 8059 7403

This is an accredited college of Southampton University but applications are made directly to the college. Psychology is studied as a combined BA/BSc Honours under a modular scheme.

LEEDS, TRINITY & ALL SAINTS COLLEGE

Leeds, Trinity & All Saints College, University of Leeds, Horsforth, Leeds LS18 5HD
Tel: 0113 283 7123

Psychology and forensic psychology are studied as a single Honours subject or in combination with marketing, management, media, human resource management, public relations, journalism, sports and exercise, nutrition and health or sociology (either as a joint Honours degree or major/minor combination). Both single and combined Honours graduates are eligible for the Graduate Basis for Registration with the BPS. The Department of Psychology has a range of dedicated laboratories and interview/observation suites. In the final year, students have the opportunity to apply their skills and knowledge by conducting an individual research project. Specialised options include: mental health and counselling psychology; health psychology; occupational psychology; forensic psychology and child psychology.

LEEDS UNIVERSITY

School of Psychology, University of Leeds, Leeds LS2 9JT
Tel: 0113 343 5724

The School of Psychology is centrally located on the University precinct. Excellent facilities are provided for both teaching and research. The School received an 'excellent' rating for the quality of its teaching in the QAA Subject Review in November 2000, and a grade 5 in the 2001 Research Assessment Exercise. There are approximately 50 staff members, 30 postgraduate students and 400 undergraduate students (300 single honours + 100 joint honours), with a broad selection of undergraduate and postgraduate courses. Research for the School is grouped into four main areas: BioPsychology, Human Factors and Performance, Health Psychology and Psychological Therapies.

LEICESTER UNIVERSITY

University of Leicester, University Road, Leicester LE1 7RH
Tel: 0116 252 2522

The headquarters of the BPS is situated in Leicester and maintains close links with the department. The research and teaching facilities include two large computer laboratories, a video laboratory, a psychometric test library and a music research library. Research strengths are concentrated in cognitive psychology, clinical psychology, forensic psychology, occupational psychology, social behaviour, development and neuroscience. BScs are also available in Psychology with a designated subsidiary subject. At present these are degrees in Psychology with: Sociology, Biology and Neuroscience. All degrees offered have graduate recognition status from the BPS.

LINCOLN UNIVERSITY

University of Lincoln, Brayford Pool, Lincoln LN6 7TS
Tel: 01522 882000

There are three psychology programmes – two single Honours programmes; Psychology, and Psychology with Clinical Psychology, and the Psychology major programme. The Psychology with Clinical Psychology programme follows the single Honours Psychology degree programme with additional compulsory units in clinical psychology at all three levels. The Psychology major is the programme followed by joint students. Psychology can be studied in combination with a wide range of subjects, including criminology, management, health studies and social policy. All three programmes cover the core areas of psychology supported by units on research methods, information technology, statistics and data analysis. On the final year of the Psychology single Honours programme, students have a wide choice of specialist topics to choose from. The programmes are accredited by the BPS.

LIVERPOOL HOPE UNIVERSITY COLLEGE

Liverpool Hope University College, Hope Park, Liverpool L16 9JD
Tel: 0151 291 3000

An approved BPS programme, Psychology is offered within the BA/BSc combined modular degree. A wide variety of final year options are offered including crime, peace, organisational, counselling and parapsychology. Facilities within the department include observation and perception laboratories. Hope has a commitment to provide a quality learning experience for all students and, to enhance this, the department has an active staff/student committee. The main Hope campus is located in a leafy suburb, a few miles from the city centre. Liverpool Hope is an accredited college of the University of Liverpool.

LIVERPOOL JOHN MOORES UNIVERSITY

Liverpool John Moores University, Roscoe Court, 4 Rodney Street, Liverpool L1 2TZ
Tel: 0151 2313 313

Two distinctive single Honours programmes are offered – BSc Applied Psychology and BSc Psychology and Biology. In addition, psychology is offered in joint or major/minor programmes with sport science, health, criminology, forensic science and sociology. Both single Honours programmes and degrees with Psychology as a major subject are accredited by the BPS.

All programmes cover the core areas of psychology and research methods and statistics. In the final year, students can choose from a range of specialist options, such as forensic psychology, occupational psychology, educational psychology, health psychology, cognitive neuropsychology, psychotherapy, human factors and topics in cognitive, developmental and social psychology.

LIVERPOOL UNIVERSITY

The University of Liverpool, Eleanor Rathbone Building, Bedford Street, South, Liverpool L69 7ZA
Tel: 0151 794 2957

There are three psychology programmes – BSc (Hons) Psychology (130 places); BSc (Hons) Psychology and Neuroscience (30 places) and BSc (Hons) Psychology and Health Sciences (30 places). Each of these courses has at its core the main fields and methods in psychology and is accredited as conferring eligibility for Graduate Membership of the BPS and the GBR. The department has undergone considerable expansion in the last three years. A virtual doubling of staff numbers allows tuition not only through lectures and tutorials but also via interactive experimental work, mainly in individual and small group projects.

LONDON, GOLDSMITHS

Goldsmiths College, University of London, London SE14 6NW
Tel: 020 7919 7171

This is a three-year course in which the final year offers a higher level of specialisation in selected topics including occupational psychology, cognitive psychology, neuropsychology, social psychology, psychopharmacology, psychology of consciousness and psychopathology. Opportunities for part-time study and intercalated work programmes are available within the BSc programme.

LONDON
METROPOLITAN
UNIVERSITY

Department of Psychology, City Campus, Calcutta House, Old Castle Street, London E1 7NT
Tel: 020 7320 1067

The Department of Psychology has been offering degrees in psychology for over 35 years. The department has two locations; City Campus is located in Calcutta House at the edge of the City of London and North Campus is located in Ladbroke House close to Highbury, north London.

City Campus currently offers a broad based BSc Psychology degree which confers Graduate Basis for Registration with the BPS, the first step towards eventually becoming a chartered psychologist. Level 1 provides a foundation in the core areas of psychology: cognitive, developmental and social psychology, individual differences, biological psychology and research methods. Level 2 builds on these foundations in greater depth to provide an excellent grounding in these core areas. Some level 1 modules also provide general support for the transition to higher education as well as teaching skills and techniques that are specific to the discipline of psychology. Experimental work at level 1 is conducted in a class context and at level 2 in small groups. At level 3 students undertake an independent research project and select specialist options from a broad range of psychology, eg abnormal psychology, atypical development, environmental psychology, cross cultural psychology, as well as advanced options in cognitive, social, biological and developmental psychology. Students also have the opportunity to select more vocationally oriented options such as forensic, health and occupational psychology that reflect the extensive portfolio of professional expertise and postgraduate courses available at City Campus.

The department also offers the BSc Applied Psychology degree at North Campus. However, this does NOT confer the Graduate Basis for Registration with the BPS, but is suitable for applicants who do not wish to pursue a career as a professional psychologist. Any potential student who is contemplating a future career in psychology is strongly advised to apply for the BSc Psychology degree.

LONDON, ROYAL HOLLOWAY

Royal Holloway, University of London, Egham Hill, Egham, Surrey TW20 0EX
Tel: 01784 434455

The Psychology Department has links with hospitals, schools and businesses which can be especially useful for the experimental project carried out in the second and third years. There is a newly built teaching laboratory and good facilities including a state-of-the-art MRI scanner (cost over £1,000,000), physiological recording equipment, and closed circuit TV and radio. The single Honours BSc Psychology course leads to GBR, as do the joint degrees combining Psychology with Mathematics or with Music. At third year level, students have a wide choice of courses, all of which are taught by leading experts in their respective areas.

LONDON, UNIVERSITY COLLEGE

UCL, Gower Street, London WC1E 6BT
Tel: 020 7679 2000

One of the first British laboratories in experimental psychology was established at UCL in 1897 and it was here in 1901 that the BPS was inaugurated. The department is now the largest department of psychology in the UK and is a major centre for psychological research with strengths in vision, cognition, neuropsychology and clinical psychology. Its experimental work is supported by three research councils and many other research-oriented bodies. The BSc single Honours degree in Psychology is accredited by the BPS and confers its GBR. During the first two years, students study all aspects of the subject and take course units outside the department. Laboratory work in the second year involves students designing and conducting their own experiments in small groups which provides a basis for the final year project. In the final year, in addition to the compulsory research project, students may study a variety of courses such as occupational psychology, language and cognition, visual perception, social psychology, theory of mind, etc. All candidates to whom places are offered are interviewed (overseas applicants excepted).

LOUGHBOROUGH
UNIVERSITY

Loughborough University, Loughborough, Leicestershire
LE11 3TU
Tel: 01509 263171

There are two distinct Psychology programmes offered at
Loughborough University – Human Psychology and Social
Psychology.

HUMAN PSYCHOLOGY
The Human Psychology Department offers multidisciplinary study
in biology, ergonomics, psychology and psychology with
ergonomics. An important feature of the psychology programme is
its situation within this well-established multidisciplinary
department. Research and teaching are both highly respected – in
the most recent Teaching Quality Review the Department achieved
24 out of 24, and its research was awarded a score of 4/5.

Both Psychology and Psychology with Ergonomics degrees fulfil the
requirements for Graduate Basis for Registration and Graduate
membership of the BPS, whilst the Psychology with Ergonomics
degree is also recognised for professional membership of the
Ergonomics Society.

The relationship between theory and application is a concern that
runs through all the programmes. Students are encouraged from
the outset to consider the relevance of psychology and to become
involved in academic work that informs and develops its critical use
and application. To achieve this, the programme is entirely oriented
towards the study of human beings. The organisation of the degree
content into modular topics also allows the opportunity of
participating in subjects elsewhere in the Department and
University. This allows students to tailor their degree programme to
their developing interests and career choices.

SOCIAL PSYCHOLOGY
The Social Psychology course in the Department of Social Sciences
was created in 1974 for students wishing to study psychology from
a social rather than a biological perspective. The course covers the
main topics of psychology, including laboratory work, and also
offers modules in such topics as sexuality, crime, psychopathology
and prejudice. Students may take modules from the other

disciplines within the department sociology, media and communications and social policy. The course is recognised by the BPS for Graduate Membership of the Society and for the GBR. The Department of Social Sciences was awarded 23 out of 24 points in its last Teaching Quality Review, and in December 2001 was designated 5 – A (a top rating) for its research expertise.

LUTON UNIVERSITY	Luton University, Park Square, Luton, Bedfordshire LU1 3JU Tel: 01582 734111

The Department of Psychology was established in 1993 in the Faculty of Health and Social Science. In the ensuing period of rapid growth and high student demand, standards have been externally endorsed as 'excellent' in the teaching of psychology, with the provision of first rate accommodation for both teaching and research. The department offers a range of undergraduate BSc (Hons) degree courses in Psychology, Health Psychology and Cultural Psychology. Cultural Psychology is the first course of its kind in the UK. Many students also choose to study Psychology with Criminology. Providing that prescribed pathways are followed, all of the above courses confer the GBR with the BPS. The department also now offers a range of part-time CertHE courses through which students can negotiate their learning with the opportunity for named routes, eg child psychology. There are many other alternatives dependent upon modules studied.

MANCHESTER METROPOLITAN UNIVERSITY	Manchester Metropolitan University, All Saints, Manchester M15 6BH Tel: 0161 247 2000

The department offers a unique range of courses, providing a comprehensive and integrated study of the fundamental areas of the discipline, and the opportunity to specialise. All courses listed here are BPS recognised as providing the GBR. The major course is the three-year BSc degree course in Psychology with the opportunity for named routes (in, for instance, criminology). There is also a combined Honours degree, allowing psychology to be studied as a major along with a wide range of other subjects. There is also a four-year degree in Psychology and Speech Pathology, which is recognised also by the Royal College of Speech and Language Therapists, thereby providing graduates with a dual qualification. Opportunities exist for part of the course to be spent elsewhere in Europe, Australia or the USA.

MMU CHESHIRE AT ALSAGER

Manchester Metropolitan University, Department of Humanities and Applied Social Studies, Hassall Road, Alsager, Cheshire ST7 2HL
Tel: 0161 247 2000

Psychology is part of the joint Honours provision at MMU Cheshire.

You may take Psychology for the award of a BA/BSc joint Honours (in combination with another subject). In this programme you need to take at least three units per year in Psychology. You may also take Psychology for the award of BA/BSc joint Honours as part of the Applied Social Studies subject pattern (in combination with another subject). In the final year of Applied Social Studies you must undertake an Independent Project equivalent to two taught units; this project may be grounded in Psychology.

There is also the opportunity to undertake a programme in the Psychology of Sport and Exercise.

This programme is designed to meet the needs of those who intend to pursue a future career in the psychology of Sport and Exercise. The programme is a joint venture between the Department of Humanities and Applied Social Studies and the Department of Exercise and Sport Science within the Faculty. Consequently students will study fundamental concepts within psychology with an emphasis upon sport and exercise science. You are encouraged to explore the relationship between theory and practice and to appreciate the application of psychological principles to sport exercise.

MANCHESTER UNIVERSITY

University of Manchester, Oxford Road, Manchester M13 9PL
Tel: 0161 275 2585

The department was established in 1919 and was the first in Great Britain to appoint a full-time Professor of Psychology. The majority of students work towards a BA or BSc Psychology degree that consists of three years. There are no differences between the two courses and the two titles only exist for historical reasons. There is also a joint degree in Psychology and Neuroscience. The neuroscience element covers a range of relevant biological topics as well as neurobiology. Psychology may be studied as an option as part of the BA combined studies in Art or BA in Human Communication but these are not recognised by the BPS.

MIDDLESEX UNIVERSITY

Middlesex University, White Hart Lane, London N17 8HR
Tel: 020 8411 5000

The Psychology degree at Middlesex University was one of the first in the UK to recognised by the BPS.

Formats of study include a single Honours degree, specialised programmes such as Psychology with Criminology or Psychology, Sport and Performance, or as a major/minor subject combined with another discipline. By choosing an appropriate mix of core and optional modules students can follow a pathway that not only appeals to their interests but is recognised by the BPS and provides an excellent foundation to the many career choices available within psychology. There is also the opportunity to undertake a sandwich degree which incorporates a work placement providing students with the opportunity to gain experience in several different areas including clinical, occupational, forensic, health and educational psychology. Students opting for the Sandwich degree also earn a Diploma in Occupational Studies.

NEWCASTLE UNIVERSITY

University of Newcastle upon Tyne, 6 Kensington Terrace, Newcastle upon Tyne NE1 7RU
Tel: 0191 222 6000

Newcastle offers psychology degrees with BPS accreditation and also joint Honours Psychology with Statistics, Computer Science, or Mathematics. Honours in Combined Studies allows Psychology with a wide range of other subjects and can also lead to BPS accreditation.

NORTHAMPTON
UNIVERSITY
COLLEGE

UCN, Broughton Green Road, Northampton NN2 7AL
Tel: 01604 735500

Students at UCN can study psychology as a single Honours subject
or as part of a combined Honours programme which enables them
to study psychology as a major, minor or joint subject. Empirical
investigation is integral to all the psychology courses, and there is
progression through each degree towards specialist final year
options. These include clinical psychology, parapsychology, forensic
psychology and neuropsychology. Students who have followed
specified pathways are eligible for GBR with the BPS.

NORTHUMBRIA
UNIVERSITY

University of Northumbria at Newcastle, Ellison Building, Ellison
Place, Newcastle upon Tyne NE1 8ST
Tel: 0191 232 6002

The Psychology degree has a substantial practical component and
includes basic training in research methods, supervised practical
classes, training in the use of standardised tests and a substantial
final-year research project. It is also possible to study psychology in
combination with sport science. All these degrees are recognised by
the BPS as conferring the GBR as a Chartered Psychologist.

NOTTINGHAM
TRENT
UNIVERSITY

The Faculty of Economic and Social Science, The Nottingham Trent
University, Burton Street, Nottingham NG1 4BU
Tel: 0115 848 5628

Psychology with BPS recognition is offered both as a single
Honours BSc degree course, and as multidisciplinary programmes
with one of criminology, sport science or one of the social sciences
(currently sociology or politics).

The programmes cover a range of approaches to psychology, with
an emphasis on behavioural science; the first two years provide a
strong foundation whilst the third year offers a choice and the
possibility of specialisation. Research methods, data analysis and
applications of psychology run throughout all versions of the
degree.

OXFORD UNIVERSITY

University of Oxford, Admissions Office, Wellington Square, Oxford OX1 2JD
Tel: 01865 270000

You can study Psychology at Oxford in two ways: either as a part subject in the joint Honours school with Philosophy and/or Physiology, or as a subject on its own in Experimental Psychology. Either route can qualify for BPS GBR. Decisions on selection are made by individual colleges, not by the Department of Experimental Psychology. You should choose a college which has a tutor in Psychology (not available at Exeter, Keble, Lincoln, Mansfield, Merton, St Peter's or Trinity). The first two terms consist of three introductory courses. You will then be examined at the end of your second term (an examination called Prelims) which allows you to move on to Part 1 (core courses) and Part 2 (options) of the Final Honours School.

PAISLEY UNIVERSITY

University of Paisley, Paisley PA1 2BE
Tel: 0141 848 3000

The Psychology Sciences programme can be taken over three years for a BA or four years for a BA Honours. The programme helps students use the findings, theories and methods of psychology to explore and understand life in contemporary society. In the final year you can choose 'elective' modules from across the University, in addition to the core elements of the programme. Paisley offers a comprehensive personal tutorial system and provides courses geared towards specific careers or postgraduate study. The degree is recognised by the BPS as conferring GBR.

PLYMOUTH UNIVERSITY

University of Plymouth, Drake Circus, Plymouth PL4 8AA
Tel: 01752 600600

There are opportunities to study psychology as a single or joint degree and to obtain work experience under two different routes. The first way is through the Visits Programme in which students attend an organisation that does work relevant to psychology. Attendance is for one half-day per week for one semester. This programme is the first of its kind in the UK. The second route is

through a sandwich placement year. Successful completion of the year entitles you to the Certificate of Industrial and Professional Experience.

PORTSMOUTH UNIVERSITY

University of Portsmouth, Winston Churchill Avenue, Portsmouth PO1 2UP
Tel: 023 9284 6313

The Department of Psychology offers a single Honours BSc in Psychology, combined Honours BSc in Psychology with Criminology and several other Honours degrees with psychology as a minor. These degrees are delivered over three years with two semesters per year, but may also be taken on a part-time basis over six years. The Psychology BSc emphasises a 'hands-on' approach to the subject and encourages links with ongoing staff research. The department has well-equipped laboratory facilities and current research interests include: child witnesses; police interviewing; primate communication; colour perception; the detection of deception; ecological approaches to intentionality; social understanding and locomotion; psychophysiology and neuropsychology.

QUEEN MARGARET COLLEGE

Queen Margaret College, Clerwood Terrace, Edinburgh EH12 8TS
Tel: 0131 317 3000

Queen Margaret University College is situated in Edinburgh. Degrees are offered over three or four years; the three year option provides an Ordinary degree. Psychology can be studied at Honours level; either as a single Honours degree (BSc (Hons) Psychology), or specialising in Health Psychology (BSc (Hons) Health Psychology), over four years. It is also possible to include Psychology as part of the joint degrees scheme, either as a major, joint or minor subject, with eg Sociology and Social Policy, or Business and Marketing. Success at Honours level in any of the awards confers eligibility for Graduate Membership of the BPS Graduate Basis for Registration. Health Psychology is a particular speciality at QMUC, although staff have a wide variety of in

SHEFFIELD UNIVERSITY

University of Sheffield, Western Bank, Sheffield S10 2TN
Tel: 0114 225 5555

The Psychology Division in the Faculty of Development and Society has approximately 400 undergraduate students on a three-year Psychology course with BPS accreditation. Special strengths of the course are cognitive, developmental and social psychology, with particular emphasis on applied psychology in the third year. There are joint courses in Psychology/Criminology, Psychology/Law and Psychology/Sociology, as well as postgraduate diplomas to enable graduates in other disciplines to secure BPS accreditation. Students come from all over the country with a range of qualifications and backgrounds.

SOUTH BANK UNIVERSITY LONDON

South Bank University, 103 Borough Road, London SE1 0AA
Tel: 020 7928 8989

The psychology division in the Faculty of Arts and Humanities and Social Sciences is an expanding unit which is active in research. Interests include speech and language difficulties, developmental psychology, social psychology, gender and sexuality, cross-cultural psychology and Applied Psychology. London South Bank offers Psychology as a single Honours or combined Honours degree programme. Students on the single Honours programme study core areas of psychology during their first two years and select a range of specialist psychology options in their third year. Combined Honours Psychology may be studied with any one of a wide range of other fields, including Criminal Studies and Forensic Science, in a minor/joint/major structure. All psychology courses, except the minor, are currently recognised by the BPS as conferring the GBR.

SOUTHAMPTON INSTITUTE

Southampton Institute, East Park Terrace, Southampton SO14 0YN
Tel: 023 8031 9000

The Human Science and Communications Department has offered a single Honours BSc in Psychology since 1996. The focus of the course is the study of mind and behaviour with coverage of the major topic areas within the field of psychology (biological, cognitive, social, developmental and individual differences approaches) as well as research methodology, quantitative and qualitative analysis and some related disciplines such as sociology. There is an emphasis throughout the course, and especially within the third year, on the application of psychology to real world issues.

SOUTHAMPTON UNIVERSITY

University of Southampton, Highfield, Southampton S017 1BJ
Tel: 02380 592619

The Psychology Department has recently achieved a grade of 5 in the Research Assessment Exercise and has enjoyed a period of expansion and now has six research groups – clinical psychology, cognitive psychology, developmental psychology, health psychology, learning and behaviour psychology, and social psychology. Students study a single Honours BSc in Psychology with BPS accreditation and graduates are eligible to apply for GBR.

STAFFORDSHIRE UNIVERSITY

Staffordshire University, College Road, Stoke-on-Trent ST4 2DE
Tel: 01782 294643

A single Honours Psychology programme is offered, as well as combined Honours Psychology with other subjects and an Honours degree in Psychology and Criminology. All programmes are approved as giving the GBR. Psychology at Stafford has received an 'excellent' assessment for its educational provision from the Quality Assurance Agency for Higher Education – scoring maximum grades in five of six categories. The courses offer a very wide range of applied psychology options in the final year of study. Staff are active in research across many different fields of psychology.

STIRLING UNIVERSITY

The University of Stirling, Stirling FK9 4LA
Tel: 01786 467640

At the University of Stirling the approach to psychology is an empirical one. An emphasis is placed on practical work from the beginning of year 1. Combined degree programmes are available across a range of disciplines (currently 14 in total). Both single and combined Honours students are automatically eligible for graduate registration with the BPS. A wide range of study electives are available, including neuro-psychology, environmental and evolutionary psychology, and community psychology. The department was rated 'excellent' in the Teaching Quality Assessment and has achieved a grade 5 (out of 5) in the recent Research Assessment Exercise.

STRATHCLYDE UNIVERSITY

University of Strathclyde, Richmond Street, Glasgow G1 1XQ
Tel: 0141 552 4400

In the first year, psychology may be chosen as one of five subjects selected from a broad range of classes in arts, social sciences and business studies. Students can then choose psychology and one other subject and continue their study in the second and third years. In the fourth year psychology may be studied to single or joint Honours levels. Admission to psychology classes in both the second year and the Honours year is selective. The department has particular strengths in the areas of social psychology, developmental and educational psychology, occupational and health psychology, perceptual-motor skills, neuropsychology, psychology of language and human communication, psychology and C&IT, interactive learning, and road-user behaviour.

SUNDERLAND UNIVERSITY

University of Sunderland, Edinburgh Building, Chester Road, Sunderland SR1 3SD
Tel: 0191 515 3000

You can choose to take pure psychology or study the discipline along with a social science. On completion of any programme you will be able to achieve Graduate Basis for Registration with the BPS. This can then point you towards a specialist field of psychology for which you can pursue a professional qualification.

The Psychology programmes at Sunderland will enable you to explore the human mind, theories of human psychology and behaviour within the related field of criminology, human society, human thought and behavioural patterns.

Other modules of study available are: child development, occupational psychology, personality, crime and criminology, dying and bereavement and sociology.

A one year study abroad placement is available in year three, particularly in Europe, North America, Australia, Japan and China. The University Language Scheme is also available to all students offering French, Spanish, Russian, Japanese, Chinese and German.

UNIVERSITY OF SURREY

University of Surrey, Guildford GU2 5XH
Tel: 01483 628885

This is a four-year course in which the third year is organised around a period of professional placements so that the students have direct experience of the practical applications of psychology. It enables them to bring this experience back to the university and apply it to final year studies. There are also extensive international links with the United States or as an ERASMUS student in France, Italy or Spain. Surrey also offers a four-year BSc in Applied Psychology and Sociology that stresses the integration of theory to practice whether it be industry, urban development, social welfare, health or education.

SUSSEX UNIVERSITY

University of Sussex, Falmer, Brighton, Sussex BN1 9RH
Tel: 01273 678416

There is the choice of a BA in Applied Psychology where there is an emphasis on applying psychology to practical problems, a BA in Developmental Psychology, a BSc in Sociology and Social Psychology as well as the normal BA or BSc in Psychology. There are many courses on offer and links with the Cognitive Science Department.

TEESSIDE UNIVERSITY

University of Teesside, Middlesborough, Cleveland TS1 3BA
Tel: 01642 218121

This three-year BSc course places an emphasis on 'hands-on' research experience through laboratory research classes. Core modules include foundations of psychology, biopsychology, perception, cognitive psychology, social psychology and developmental psychology.

THAMES
VALLEY
UNIVERSITY

Thames Valley University, St Mary's Road, Ealing, London W5 5RF
Tel: 0800 036 8888

The specialist BSc (Hons) Psychology course at Thames Valley University (TVU) is one of the longest established psychology courses in the UK and is accredited as conferring eligibility for Graduate Membership of the BPS, and the Graduate Basis for Registration. The course includes a placement, during which students will have the opportunity to analyse the relationship between psychological theory and practice, and to gain experience of applying psychological understanding in a health, community or research setting.

TVU also offers BA (Hons) Psychology, and a BSc (Hons) Psychology with Counselling Theory. All of the courses allow students to gain a full grounding and explore the process of psychological research.

ULSTER
UNIVERSITY

University of Ulster, Cromore Road, Coleraine, County Londonderry, Northern Ireland BT52 1SA
Tel: 08 700 400 700

Ulster offers a course in BSc Applied Psychology at its Jordanstown campus (near Belfast) with an 18-week work placement in the third year. Students may spend their placement outside Northern Ireland. The majority of placements are located in Great Britain and the Republic of Ireland. At its Coleraine campus on the North Coast, Ulster offers a BSc (Hons) in Social Psychology and a BSc (Hons) in Social Psychology and Sociology, both with short periods of work placements or a full one year placement available on a competitive basis. At the Magee campus in the historic city of Derry, Ulster offers a BSc (Hons) in Psychology which includes a short work placement. All of Ulster's psychology degrees confer GBR by the BPS.

WALES
(BANGOR)

The University of Wales, Bangor, Gwynedd LL57 3DG
Tel: 01248 351151

The most recent official assessments of research and teaching showed the School of Psychology at Bangor to be among the leading departments in the country. Facilities include a Student Learning Resource Centre, a Macintosh Laboratory with over 100 machines for student use, and a day nursery in which child behaviour can be observed first hand. Teaching is carried out in a flexible and student-oriented manner, supported by the latest technology. Areas of research include learning language and development, cognitive psychology and neuroscience, clinical and health psychology and experimental consumer psychology. Undergraduates take a BA or BSc degree (with no difference in course content) and may read for Honours in either Psychology, Psychology with Clinical and Health Psychology, Psychology with Neuropsychology or Psychology with Child and Language Development. All of these single Honours courses carry full BPS accreditation.

UNIVERSITY OF
WALES
INSTITUTE
CARDIFF

UWIC, Llandaff Campus, Western Avenue, Cardiff CF5 2YB
Tel: 029 2041 7011

UWIC offers a full-time, modular psychology degree (BSc Hons Psychology), recognised by the BPS for the GBR. In the first year, students are introduced to core psychology subjects which are developed over the following two years. In the third year of the course, students have the opportunity to select option modules that reflect their interests in psychology or the careers that they wish to follow. In addition, third year students undertake their own research on a psychology topic for their under graduate project. Assessed coursework and examinations take place in all three years. All modules must be passed to gain a degree, but the degree classification depends on the results from the second and third years of the course. The degree is validated by the University of Wales.

**WALES
(SWANSEA)**

University of Wales, Swansea, Singleton Park, Swansea SA2 8PP
Tel: 01792 205678

Psychology at Swansea can be studied as a single subject or as a pair
of subjects in the Faculty of Arts and Social Studies or Sciences.
Joint Honours include Psychology with Law, Sociology, Social
Anthropology, Economics, Philosophy, Biology and Computer
Science, Criminology, Russian, Spanish, Welsh, German, French
and Italian.

**UNIVERSITY OF
WARWICK**

University of Warwick, Coventry CV4 7AL
Tel: 02476 523723

Warwick offers a single Honours BSc in Psychology and a joint
Honours BSc in Psychology and Philosophy. Both these degrees
confer eligibility for Graduate Membership of the BPS and GBR as
a Chartered Psychologist. The single Hons BSc is a three-year
programme offering a general grounding in methodology and the
principal areas of Psychology. Thus a quarter of the degree credit
comes from practical and project work, with the remainder coming
from courses in biological, cognitive, developmental, social and
abnormal psychology. The first two years consist of core courses in
these areas, enabling the third year to contain a core project and a
choice of six options from a list of about twelve. Assessment comes
from exams (50%) with the remaining 50% coming from essays,
project reports, presentations and tests. The joint Honours
Psychology and Philosophy programme places constraints on the
number and range of psychology courses taken to ensure BPS
requirements are met. Further details can be obtained from the
web at http://www2.warwick.ac.uk/fac/sci/psych/ .

**WESTMINSTER
UNIVERSITY**

University of Westminster, 309 Regent Street, London W1B 2UW
Tel: 020 7911 5088

BSc Psychology is a single Honours degree offered at Regent
Campus in central London. The course provides coverage of core
areas of the discipline of Psychology, while the option modules deal
with areas of application of psychological theory and research and
give insight into the practice of psychology in a range of settings.

Core modules such as Social and Developmental Psychology, Personality Psychobiology, Individual Differences and Developmental Psychology are taken within the first and second year. There is a choice of applied areas in the third year including Cognitive Disorders, Forensic Psychology, Business Psychology and Health Psychology. The course can be taken full or part time. The University also offers a BSc Psychological Sciences and BSc in Cognitive Sciences. All three degrees are accredited by the BPS as conferring the Graduate Basis for Registration.

WOLVERHAMPTON UNIVERSITY

The University of Wolverhampton, Wulfruna Street, Wolverhampton WV1 1SB
Tel: 01902 321000

Wolverhampton offers three-year degree courses, all accredited for GBR by the BPS. These courses cover the core areas within the BPS curriculum, whilst allowing you to develop areas of personal interest, and enable you to develop your skills as an independent learner and a critical thinker. All courses are available full time or part time.

BSc Hons Psychology
BSc Hons Psychology in Combined Awards
BSc Hons Sport and Exercise Psychology
BSc Hons Work, Occupational and Organizational Psychology
BSc Hons Counselling Psychology

WORCESTER UNIVERSITY COLLEGE

University College Worcester, Henwick Grove, Worcester WR2 6AJ
Tel: 01905 855000

Students may follow either a single Honours, major, joint, or minor pathway in Psychology. Those graduating with a single, major or joint degree will be eligible to apply for Graduate Membership of the BPS. Those who follow a specified route through the single Honours and major pathway will be eligible to apply for Graduate Membership with GBR of the BPS. Psychology combines well with health studies, business management, biological science, sociology and education studies. The department has specific research interests in the areas of social psychology, occupational psychology, developmental psychology and gerontology and offers an MSc in Gerontology. Other Masters courses are currently being developed.

UNIVERSITY OF YORK

The University of York, Heslington, York YO10 5DD
Tel: 01904 430000

York's BSc Honours Psychology degree offers an overall coverage of the subject with particular emphasis on psychology as an experimental science and academic discipline. After studying all major areas of psychology in the first two years, students have a large range of advanced options from which to choose.

YORK ST JOHN

York St John, College of the University of Leeds, Lord Mayor's Walk, York YO31 7EX
Tel: 01904 624624

Psychology is available as a single Honours degree. Tutors have backgrounds in applied psychology and are dedicated to teaching and research in psychology. Psychology is also available in a joint Honours programme combined with a variety of subjects.

FURTHER INFORMATION

USEFUL
ADDRESSES

BRITISH PSYCHOLOGICAL SOCIETY
The British Psychological Society (BPS) is the professional
association for psychologists and is incorporated by Royal
Charter. A Register of Chartered Psychologists was established in
1987, bringing a more organised and stricter discipline to the
profession. Chartered Psychologists are bound to an ethical code
of conduct which was set up to maintain the standards of
psychology as a profession and to protect the public. The Society
publishes a useful pamphlet 'So you want to be a Psychologist' –
essential reading for prospective psychologists – and a range of
information leaflets.

The Register contains members of the Society who have reached a
certain standard in education and work experience. It contains their
names, qualifications and work addresses. Copies of the Register
can be found at main public reference libraries and at professional
organisations and certain employer bodies.

The Register is split into specialist areas such as clinical,
criminological and legal, educational, occupational and counselling
psychology.

To qualify for registration as a Chartered Psychologist you must:

■ have completed a first qualification in psychology that is a Graduate Basis for Registration (GBR);

■ have undergone a further course or supervised training in a specific area of psychology;

■ have agreed to abide by a Code of Conduct laid down by the British Psychology Society;

■ be judged fit to practise psychology without supervision.

For further information contact:

The British Psychological Society, St Andrews House, 48 Princess Road East, Leicester LE1 7DR.
www.bps.org.uk

The British Association of Sport and Exercise Sciences (BASES), Chelsea Close, Armley, Leeds LS12 4HP.
www.bases.org.uk

UK Council for Psychotherapy, 167–169 Great Portland Street, London W1W 5PF.
Tel: 020 7436 3002

The Association of Educational Psychologists, 26 The Avenue, Durham DH1 4ED.
www.aep.org.uk

The British Association for Counselling and Psychotherapy, Regent Place, Rugby, Warwickshire CV21 2PJ.
www.bacp.co.uk

GENERAL UNIVERSITY GUIDES

CRAC Degree Course Guides (Psychology), published by Trotman & Co. Ltd.

Degree Course Offers, by Brian Heap, published annually by Trotman & Co Ltd. www.trotmanpublishing.co.uk.

Entrance Guide to Higher Education in Scotland, published by the Committee of Scottish Higher Education Principals, St Andrew House, 141 West Hill Street, Glasgow G1 2RN.

How to Complete Your UCAS Form, published annually by Trotman & Co Ltd. www.trotmanpublishing.co.uk.

The Student Book, Klaus Boehm & Jenny Lees-Spalding (eds), published annually by Trotman & Co Ltd. www.trotmanpublishing.co.uk.

The UCAS Handbook is free to UK addresses from UCAS, PO Box 28, Cheltenham, Gloucestershire GL52 3LZ. (www.ucas.com)

University and College Entrance: The Official Guide, published by UCAS (see above).

PSYCHOLOGY TEXTS

As far as specific psychology textbooks go, any of the introductory texts found in large bookshops are fine. Those relating to social psychology are probably the easiest and most interesting to read if you are new to the subject.

A User's Guide to the Brain, John Ratey, Abacus

Body Language, Allan Pease, Sheldon Press

Dictionary of Psychology, Andrew M Colman, Cambridge University Press

Emotional Intelligence, Daniel Goldman, Bloomsbury

From the Edge of the Couch, Raj Persaud, Bantam

Mapping the Mind, Rita Carter, Weidenfeld & Nicolson

Memory, David Samuel, Phoenix

The Moral Animal – The New Science of Evolutionary Psychology, Robert Wright, Abacus

The Noonday Demon – An Anatomy of Depression, Andrew Solomon, Chatto & Windus

Penguin Dictionary of Psychology, Reber and Reber, Penguin

Phobias – Fighting the Fear, Helen Saul, HarperCollins

QI – The Quest for Intelligence, Kevin Warwick, Piatkus

The Human Mind, Robert Winston, Bantam

Tomorrow's People, Susan Greenfield, Penguin

Totem and Talent, Sigmund Freud, Routledge

WEBSITES

British Psychological Society: www.bps.org.uk
Psychology Today: www.psychologytoday.com
Business Psychology News: www.businesspsychologist.com
Psych Central: www.psychcentral.com